In the wonderful world the Greks had given us

. . . unemployment was rising, but no one cared about that. Soon the Grek machines would take over all labor and nobody would need to work. People were hungry, but they tightened their belts and waited for the Greks' advanced method of fertilization to produce enough food for all.

A few people were beginning to look with horror at the new Grek-made world. They saw how the Greks' promises had destroyed ambition and incentive. They saw Earthmen, with their eyes fixed on the future, refusing to work enough to supply the needs of the present.

These doubting few banded together to resist the Greks' scheme of conquest by generosity. But they knew that even a united Earth would have a hard time fighting the advanced technology of the Greks. What chance was there for a handful of people, with no army and no weapons?

About the author:

Murray Leinster has been called the "Dean of Science Fiction" because his first science fiction story appeared way back in 1920. Since then he has written countless other short stories and books in the field, has won a "Hugo" (the science fiction equivalent of an Oscar), and was the guest of honor at last year's World Science Fiction Convention. In his spare time he turns his imagination to inventing. He holds several patents, two of which are for products currently in manufacture.

THE GREKS
BRING GIFTS

MURRAY LEINSTER

MB
A MACFADDEN-BARTELL BOOK

A MACFADDEN BOOK

First printing . . . . December, 1964
Second printing . . . . February, 1968

THIS IS A MACFADDEN ORIGINAL
NEVER BEFORE PUBLISHED IN BOOK FORM

MACFADDEN BOOKS are published by
Macfadden-Bartell Corporation
A subsidiary of Bartell Media Corporation
205 East 42nd Street, New York, New York, 10017.

The
Greks
Bring
Gifts

1

WE WHO remember the coming of the Greks find it
hard to explain to a later generation just how terrifying that coming was, and why we acted as we did.
After all, even at the beginning and for a really considerable time, the Greks made no menacing move.
Their ship simply came casually around the edge of
the moon and moved off some thousands of miles to
one side. Then it stopped. It lay there motionless in
space, as if looking us over and debating what to do
about us, or with us. It could not be said that the ship
made any alarming move or gave any evidence of un-
toward intentions. But we had hysterics.

Mainly, perhaps, that was because the Grek ship was
monstrous. It was fully a quarter of a mile long, and
thick in proportion. It glittered with a total-reflection
surface material which kept it from either radiating
heat to the emptiness of between-the-stars, or from
absorbing heat when close to a white-hot sun. It was
huge beyond imagining. We humans had sent probes
to Mars and Venus, but we hadn't yet landed a working party on the moon. The only space drive we could
imagine was rockets, and we'd gotten rockets to do
about all they could. Which wasn't much. Until we
saw the Grek ship, we couldn't conceive of anything
as gigantic, as powerful, and as deadly as that seemed
to be.

So when the ship did appear, and lay still in space
apparently considering what to make of Earth and its
quaint aborigines, we gibbered. We felt that if there
were another intelligent race in our galaxy, it must
be made in the image and likeness of men. And if
we'd been able to build a ship like the Grek one, and
if we'd found a world like Earth, we'd have taken it

7

over. If it had a primitive race in residence on it, we'd
have enslaved or massacred them.

Naturally, then, we expected the Greks to act as we
would have done in their place. So we had hysterics.
But if we'd known from the beginning what we found
out later, hysterics wouldn't have begun to express
our feelings!

At that, though, we were lucky. The Greks could
have arrived half a century earlier, before the idea of
broadcasting had been thought of and applied. We'd
have been much worse off if newspapers had been the
only way to distribute information. In other ways we
were even luckier. One of the strangest ways was the
good fortune we had in Jim Hackett. He was old
enough to have been nominated for a Nobel Prize in
physics, and young enough to have been refused it because of his youth. But apparently nobody thought of
him at all. Certainly not as a piece of good luck.

At the moment we couldn't imagine good luck in
any form. On all of Earth hysteria succeeded hysterics.
There were financial panics in all the civilized countries. Some people seemed to think that if Earth were
to be destroyed or conquered by creatures from outer
space, it would somehow be useful to have money
credits in soundly managed banks. There were political crises, as if who was in office would matter if all
human government—or humanity itself—were to be
abolished. And, of course, great numbers of people
tried to flee the cities in the belief that there would be
greater safety where there were fewer numbers. This
however, may have been true.

Meanwhile the Grek ship lay perfectly still in space.
It made no move. It sent no signals. It showed no signs
of life. Ultimately, that quietness had its effect. From
crazy and tumultuous rioting, which had many cities
in flames and turned loose death and destruction everywhere, things calmed down a little. As nobody knew
how the riots had started nobody knew how they happened to stop. But in eighteen hours there was relative
order again. We were no less frightened, but we'd become bewildered. We calmed to mere desperation. For

the first time in three generations there was practically
no tension in international affairs. The heads of government communicated in a common funk that allowed
of sincerity. The danger was equal for all nations. So
presently there was a shaky, jittering alliance of all
the world against the Grek ship. Which remained
motionless.

Things couldn't go on in that state, obviously, so we
attempted to make contact with the ship from beyond
the stars. The attempts ranged from the idiotic to the
absurd. An effort was made to open up two-way conversations by sending sequences of microwave pulses
which said explicitly that two times two is four, and
two times three is six, and so on to more rarefied math-
ematical conversation, such as a witticism about nine
times twelve. There were attempts to communicate by
means of television signals to the neighborhood of the
moon, to inform the Greks—we didn't know that name
yet—that we called ourselves men, that we were civilized, that we conversed by sounds, and that this sound
meant this object and that sound that. Not less than
twelve different languages were used by different people trying this process, but—somehow there came a
breakthrough.

Two days after their first appearance, the Greks
replied. Their answer consisted of six completely un-
related words, evidently transmitted from recordings
the Greks had made of the confusions transmitted to
them. Together the words had no meaning, but they
did convey the idea that the Greks recognized them
as meaningful and invited more systematic broadcasts
on the same order.

To us, at the time, that set of six random words had
the impact of a stay of execution in a death house. The
Greks ceased to be inexplicable and terrifying, and
became merely strangers who could not speak a human
language and humbly asked to be helped to learn one.
So we immediately began to assist them.

Eventually they stopped our instructions by beaming
down a coherent and meaningful message. Nobody
knows how they learned which words meant what—

not in the case of verbs, anyhow—or how they contrived a lucid if lawless grammer. These are things we haven't found out yet. But the message arrived, and it was intelligible. It was warmly, blandly, deliciously comforting. We humans almost started to riot again out of pure relief.

The message said that the Grek ship greeted the inhabitants of this third planet out from the local sun. The ship was, so they said, a sort of school ship for spacemen of the Nurmi cluster. It trained aspirants for officers' ratings in the space merchantships of that area, where there were thousands of civilized planets. The officers and teaching faculty were members of a race called Greks, and the ship was taking a class of Aldarian student spacemen on a training voyage. It had come upon the Earth by pure accident, while giving its students an exercise in the examination of unfamiliar solar systems. It had occurred to the Grek instructors that their student crewmen would find it very educational to make contact with a new intelligent race, to pass on such technical information as might be useful, and even—if the inhabitants of Earth approved —to prepare them for a sound commercial relationship later with the worlds the Aldarians knew.

For these reasons, therefore, the Grek ship asked permission to land. It had established communication for that purpose. The Greks' intention—so they said— was purely and solely to benefit us, to make us healthy and wealthy and wise.

And we believed them! Heaven help us, we believed them!

2

EVERYBODY was comforted. Everybody was happy. Nobody would have thought, of course, that visitors from beyond the stars were do-gooders of purest ray serene. But we were desperately anxious to believe it, once the idea was suggested. More details came from

the monstrous ship. Yes, they were utterly altruistic
and wholly philanthropic. They traveled from star to
star, innocently engaged in making people happy while
they trained astrogators and engineroom officers as
benevolent as themselves. What more would we want?
How could we improve on that as bait? We couldn't.

But the Greks could. They did.

They landed their ship in Ohio in an enormous earth-
en cradle Army engineers scooped out for them. In
preparing the earth cradle, the military men thought-
fully buried four atomic fission bombs where they
would be handy if we needed them. They were arranged to be detonated from a distance. There were
also ballistic missiles with atomic warheads, prudently
placed in concealment a good way from the landing
site. They could blast even the Grek ship to incandescent, radioactive gas if the need arose. But apparently we were much ashamed of this afterward. From
the moment of their landing until after their departure,
it seems that nobody thought a single naughty thought
about the Greks. They were wonderful! They were
making everybody rich! For six months the Greks
were deliriously revered.

It is still hard for us who went through all this to
make another generation understand why we acted
and felt as we did. But now we know what the Greks
are like. Then we didn't. Now we know what they
came for. Then we were intoxicated by the gifts they
brought us. We hadn't discovered that unearned riches
are as bad for a race as for a person. And the Greks
had made us rich.

In the six months the Greks were aground we acquired broadcast power. Not yet an adequate supply
for all the waste a planet's population could achieve.
Not yet. But anybody who had a receiving unit could
draw from the air all the power he needed to light
or heat his house and run his ground car or his small-
sized business, if he had one. We had de-salting plants
turning salt water into fresh for the irrigation of the
Sahara Basin, and we anticipated having all the fresh
water we could use in all the arid regions of the world.

We had fish-herding electronic devices that drove un-
believable quantities of ocean fish into estuaries to be
netted. We had a sinter field which made the minerals
in topsoil more available to plants, and our crops promised to be unmanageably huge. We had plastics we
hadn't dreamed of, materials we could hardly believe,
and new manufacturing processes. . . .

After six months the Greks announced that they
were going away. They'd leave us to the enjoyment of
our new wealth. We owed them nothing. What they
had done had been done out of the goodness of their
hearts. True, they made most of their benefactions
through their furry Aldarian student spacemen. We
liked the Aldarians, though it was odd that they had
external ears but were totally deaf. We felt uncomfortable in the presence of Greks. The feeling Greks
produced in human beings was usually described as
"creepy." But we were grateful to them. We idolized
them. Being the kind of idiots we were, we practically
worshipped the Greks for their benefactions!

If all this seems improbable, it's true just the same.
The rest of the tale may make it believable.

The rest may as well begin with Jim Hackett on the
day before the leaving of the Greks. The date of their
departure had been proclaimed a planetary holiday,
the first in human history. All of Earth would take the
day off to do honor to those gray-skinned, bald and
uninterested creatures who had remade our world
much nearer to our hearts' desire.

At the lift-off spot itself, in Ohio, it was estimated
that not less than a million and a half human beings
would congregate to tell the Greks goodbye. In the rest
of America there were to be other gigantic farewell
parties. They'd be linked to the actual lift-off spot by
closed-circuit television. In Europe, in Asia, in Aus-
tralia, in South America, in Africa—everywhere—the
world prepared to do honor to the Greks on their departure.

In the United States, naturally, the celebration began with the worst traffic foul-up in the history of self-
propelled vehicles. And Hackett was caught in it. He

was going to the lift-off ceremony for a reason of his own. He'd made a suggestion to an archaeologist he knew, and he wanted to see what it turned up, if anything. He'd picked up Lucy Thale—she'd been Doctor Lucy Thale this past full month—at the hospital where she'd been interning. She wanted to see the Greks go away. After four hours of stop-and-go crawling, Hackett swerved off the official main highway to the lift-off site and turned onto a secondary road.

There was an enormous difference. The two-lane main road had been a solid, packed, crawling mass of vehicles. Now and again they halted by necessity. Sooner or later they started up again, to crawl at five to ten miles an hour until perforce they halted once more. When he got on the narrower road, though, Hackett could make fifty miles an hour or better.

It was a singularly perfect day, with remarkably green grass and an unusually blue sky, and little white clouds sailing overhead. This road wound and twisted, and the main highway gradually moved farther and farther away toward the horizon, until one couldn't even smell the gas fumes from its fuel-driven cars. Seven-eighths of the cars on the road were still that kind. The cars that ran on broadcast power were coming out of the factories, but there weren't anywhere near enough of them to meet the public demand. There were other difficulties about them, too. But everybody knew that everything would be ironed out shortly.

Hackett drove, thinking absorbedly to himself. Lucy Thale took a deep breath of the purer air.

"It'll be a good thing," she said, "when all cars run on broadcast power. It was stifling on the highway!"

Hackett grunted.

"It's the heaviest traffic in history. I can imagine only one way it could be heavier."

Lucy turned her head to look at him inquiringly.

"Everybody on the road," he told her, "is on the way to cheer and praise the Greks. But if they'd turned out not to be as benevolent as they seem, there'd be heavier traffic trying to get away from them."

Lucy smiled a little.

"You're not enthusiastic about the Greks, Jim."

"I'm less enthusiastic about the human race," he said grimly. "We're about in the position of the American Indians when the whites came to America. The Greks are farther ahead of us than our ancestors were ahead of the Indians. But the Indians didn't quarrel among themselves for the privilege of letting the whites destroy them!"

"But the Greks aren't—"

"Aren't they?" asked Hackett sourly.

Lucy said, "They've given us things we didn't hope to have for generations to come!"

"We gave the Indians metal tomahawks and whiskey and guns," growled Hackett. "They killed each other with the tomahawks, drank themselves to death on the whiskey, and fairly often they used the guns on us. But they didn't try to keep each other from having the guns or the tomahawks or the whiskey. We're not so tolerant."

Lucy did not comment. There were some governments which protested that it was unfair for other nations with more developed industry and more trained technical workers to be able to make more use of the Greks' gifts than they could. They argued that they should be given extra aid to lift themselves level. But so far it was only squabbling. It would be smoothed out. Everybody was sure it would work out all right.

"Also," said Hackett, "Indians didn't go hungry because flint arrowheads became obsolete. Have you seen the unemployment figures? The Indians didn't pauperize their hunters because they weren't needed while everybody was busy getting drunk! The thing hasn't hit you, Lucy. You're a doctor, and the Greks haven't made medicine a useless skill. But most of the world isn't so lucky. Me, for example."

Again Lucy did not answer. Hackett had been among the first to feel the impact of the Greks upon his career. He had been the youngest man ever to be nominated for a Nobel Prize and, though he hadn't received it, he'd had some reputation and the prospect of considerable achievements in the years to come. So he'd been included in the group of Earth physicists to whom the Greks offered instruction in their more advanced science. But he hadn't made the grade. The painstakingly translated Grek texts on physics made sense to him so far and no further. At a certain point the statements seemed to him to become meaningless gobbledygook. He couldn't follow the reasoning or grasp the ideas. They seemed simply nonsensical, leading nowhere and accounting for nothing. So the Greks, with painstaking sighs of regret, observed that he seemed incapable of the kind of thinking their sciences required, and politely showed him the door.

He hadn't taken it well. There were other physicists who went on zestfully through the most abstruse areas of Grek theory. They'd produced nothing new as yet, of course. They couldn't hope for independent achievement before they were thoroughly grounded in the new way of looking at things. But they were admired, while Hackett had lost his reputation with his dismissal. He no longer had a career. His training and his work up to now had become useless.

At this time we who were madly absorbed in the gifts the Greks had brought us couldn't see Jim's value. There were a lot of things we didn't see. We don't feel proud of ourselves. We were idiots. Some of us were worse than idiots. Very luckily, Hackett wasn't.

But he had enough reason to feel bitter as he drove along a curving secondary road on the day before the Greks' departure. Beside him, Lucy Thale frowned a little. She wasn't too happy, either. She'd just finished her year's interning at Hoyt Memorial Hospital, and she'd been debating what it would mean if she married Hackett. There'd been a time when it had seemed a complete and beautifully satisfying career. But Hackett wasn't thinking romantically now.

The traffic grew more dense even on this road. From fifty miles an hour, the practical road speed dropped to forty, then to thirty. Others beside Hackett had abandoned the toll highways for lesser thoroughfares. Hackett drove automatically, scowling to himself.

The traffic stopped. Hackett braked, and wound up with his front bumper only inches from the car ahead. Presently movement began again, inch by inch and foot by foot. A long time later they came to a place where a car had swerved out of the right-hand lane to try to leapfrog on ahead. There'd been a truck coming in the opposite direction and the leap-frogging car couldn't get back into its proper lane. It should have darted across the road into a ditch. It hadn't. A wrecked truck and four more or less wrecked cars had blocked traffic for a time. The cars had now been pushed off the highway. Traffic speeded up again.

"That's six wrecks we've seen so far today," observed Lucy. "If anybody was hurt, though—"

If so, they'd been taken away. The national highway safety board had estimated that there would be between nine hundred and a thousand highway fatalities today, due to the traffic toward the lift-off tribute to the Greks. That compared with estimates of six to seven hundred for a long Fourth of July weekend. The farewell to the Greks would be costly in human lives, but there was no way to prevent it. And Hackett had spent a good deal of his financial reserves getting tickets for himself and Lucy to watch the departure.

There were gigantic grandstands built all around the monstrous space ship. There were many square miles of parking space set aside. There were acres of cubbyholes containing bunks, to be rented for the night before the take-off. There was an enormous bunting-draped auditorium in which an incredible departure party would be held in honor of the Greks. Humanity would do itself proud. There were already organizations collecting funds with which to build a towering permanent monument where the Greks had first landed. It seemed proper. Hadn't the Greks come to turn Earth into a terrestrial paradise in which nobody would work more than a day a week, all men would retire at forty, and everybody would have every possession he'd ever envied anybody else?

It is too bad those plans for a monument weren't carried through. It might be useful to remind later generations what fools we humans can be.

The traffic spread out to where individual vehicles were one car length apart and the speed was up to fifty miles an hour once more. Small towns and villages appeared near the roadside from time to time. Little service highways led to them. Hackett noticed a car lumbering off to the right at one such turnoff. Two miles later he saw two more cars turn off. Not long after, another car went careening out of the traffic-loaded secondary road, though there was then no settlement of any sort in sight. Each of these cars seemed to turn off in consequence of something ahead of Hackett. The first one he'd noticed was perhaps the eighth car ahead. The seventh had swerved off on a lesser road. The sixth was followed off by the fifth. The road passed a small town with twin steeples on its church, and the fourth car ahead left at the next possible exit. The third and second went off together. It was peculiar.

Then the car just ahead of Hackett turned off. It would not be easy to get back into such traffic as this, but it left. And then Hackett saw what eight other cars had refused to follow. But Lucy saw it first.

"Jim!" she said quickly. "Look! It's an Aldarian!"

Hackett nodded with some grimness. The car just ahead was a convertible with its top down. It slowed violently, as if a foot had been taken off its accelerator. Hackett had to brake to avoid crashing into it. But then it shot ahead with such acceleration as almost to crash into the car ahead. It braked again and swerved wildly, came back on the highway, and proceeded normally for a minute or more. Then it darted to the right, overcorrected so it headed into the left-hand lane, and got back just before a monstrous truck roared by from the opposite direction.

The convertible stopped short and Hackett burned rubber to keep from smashing into it. Instinctively he cringed in anticipation of being crashed into from behind. But the white convertible shot ahead again and Jim sent his own car leaping after it.

"Yes," he said between his teeth, "it's an Aldarian. And he's a lousy driver. Somebody'll get killed if he keeps on!"

The furry poll and ears of an Aldarian showed above the back of the driver's seat. The world loved Aldarians—one of the few excusable reactions we managed in connection with the stay of the Grek ship. The Aldarians were likable. We owed gratitude to the Greks, but it had to be admitted that they made human beings feel creepy. Aldarians were something else again. They were, we understood, the students and trainees of the Greks. They knew vastly more than men, but one didn't feel uncomfortably inferior to them. They didn't make anybody feel creepy. And they took delight in doing primitive things—like driving human-design cars—which their Grek officers and instructors in the training ship never bothered with.

This Aldarian doubtless enjoyed driving a human car in the middle of human traffic. He'd probably been presented with it. Greks and Aldarians alike were overwhelmed with gifts everywhere they went. But he shouldn't have tried to drive in traffic like this, not until he'd had a lot of practice. His car required the constant attention of its driver, which was not true of Grek-designed cars. He couldn't remember that requirement. He was charmed with the adventure he was having. . . .

Lucy watched, fascinated by the sight of an Aldarian in the flesh. Hackett swore at his erratic driving. He not only swerved unpredictably, but from time to time he had to slow down and put his whole mind on aiming his car again. Which is not a good practice in nearly bumper-to-bumper traffic at fifty miles an hour.

Lucy said suddenly, "Jim, Aldarians are deaf, aren't they?"

"Yes, all of them." Hackett added sourly, "They're also crazy as drivers."

"But—they've got ears! Why?"

Hackett did not answer immediately. The Aldarian

driver found himself about to run off the highway to the right and agitatedly swung to the left, just as a truckload of lumber raced past in the opposite direction. The truck tapped the alien's car, at exactly the right angle and with just the right force to flip it sharply into its proper lane and line of travel. The furry-headed driver was flung to one side. He straightened up frantically, and found everything perfectly normal. He was bemused. He was astonished!

"This one," said Hackett, "seems to have a rabbit's foot in wonderful working order! But I think he's dangerous."

"But why," insisted Lucy, "would Aldarians have ears if they can't hear? How could a bodily structure develop if it didn't work? How could a creature develop ears if it made no use of sounds?"

"I don't know," said Hackett. "The question's been raised before, privately, but not in public that I know of."

There was a little group of people beside the road. Others came running to join them from the town the highway now skirted. When the white convertible with the Aldarian driver went past, the people waved wildly. They cheered. Those who ran to join them waved and shouted too. It was easy to guess that the Aldarian was driving to rejoin his ship before it lifted off. And Aldarians were infinitely popular.

Through them—the Greks stayed in their ship, mostly—everybody in the world would presently be a millionaire. Food would be so plentiful that even the lavish living standard of America would be raised. Everybody would have everything he'd ever envied the rich for having. The Greks were providing this good fortune, but the Aldarians were its distributors. People liked them! Women said gushingly that they were cute, and men felt comfortably superior because they were deaf and had to communicate by writing. And they were friendly, and helpful, and they liked humans, whereas the Greks were merely distantly polite. And they made people feel creepy.

Half a mile on, another group of people waited. They

waved and cheered as the Aldarian drove unskillfully
past them. They laughed tolerantly at his incompe-
tence. They liked him for trying to drive a human car.
They applauded. Evidently one of the turned-off cars
had telephoned ahead that an Aldarian was driving by,
and people had come out to wave or shout warm and
friendly greetings which the Aldarian could not hear.

But driving behind him was dangerous.

"It's practically a miracle," Hackett said coldly, as
the divergations of the car ahead seemed to grow
wilder, "that he hasn't crashed into something yet. But
miracles don't go on forever, Lucy. He's going to be in
the middle of a pile-up of cars presently, and I don't
want you in it. So I'm turning off at the next side
road."

"We may not be able to get back on the highway,"
she said, "but if you think we'd better—"

That was the instant it happened. An oil truck
flashed past on the other lane. It made the loudest of
possible roarings. The Aldarian's car flinched away
from it. It straightened out. Then three enormous
trucks-and-trailers went bellowing by, tailgate to
bumper. At each flashing appearance, the Aldarian
flinched again. After the last, his right-hand wheels
were off the concrete. He jerked the car crazily back
on the road and went partly into the other lane. Something monstrous and howling plunged toward him. All
his partly acquired responses went into action together.
He swerved frantically to the right, jammed down the
accelerator—

His car leaped crosswise off the road. It went into a
ditch, careened and came out of it, and then, in the act
of overturning, crashed violently into a tree.

Hackett had already reacted when the crash came.
For a long while he'd been expecting some accident.
Now he followed the white car instantly off the highway, steering with inspired accuracy. He hit the same
ditch at the exactly right angle and bounced out of it
with a monstrous crashing of springs. He had all four
wheels in the air for part of a second, but then his
car came to a grinding, locked-wheel stop not more

than five feet from where the Aldarian had been thrown partly clear.

He was out in an instant. There was the smell of gasoline. A flame licked up. He scooped up the Aldarian in his arms. Lucy opened the rear-seat door. Hackett put the Aldarian on the cushions, snapped orders to Lucy—later he didn't remember what they'd been—and she jumped in beside the curiously crumpled figure. Hackett shot his car fiercely ahead just as the white car started really to burn.

Lucy said evenly, as the car lurched and swayed on the uneven ground, "He's not bleeding that I can see, but that's all I can see."

"You're a doctor, and it's not likely any other human doctor can do more. We'll have to get him to a hospital, fast! They may have equipment that'll do some good."

He drove on, on the shoulder of the road. He could see a fence ahead which might mark a feeder road joining the highway. He made for it as swiftly as he could.

Behind him there arose a wild, sky-shattering wail. The car that had followed him blew its horn violently to warn other cars behind it that something drastic had happened. Those other cars sounded their horns, and others behind them, to the horizon, set up a dismal din. But the traffic didn't stop. Moving cars near the now fiercely burning wreck only tried to speed up to get past it. Others speeded up as space opened before them. Perhaps fewer than a dozen cars actually knew what had happened. The rest only knew that a toppled white convertible blazed on its side by the highway.

Hackett braked and stopped at a house a quarter mile from the road. He banged on a door until it opened. He snapped explanations before it was fully ajar, demanding a telephone and the nearest hospital in one breath. He got the hospital on the phone, while all the occupants of the house ran to see an actual Aldarian at close quarters. While Hackett telephoned, Lucy made careful, tentative efforts to make the injured alien more comfortable.

Hackett came out. "There'll be motor cops coming

to meet us," he said. "They're getting X-rays ready at the hospital, and they're getting in touch with the Grek ship, asking what to do first. There'll probably be a helicopter coming to take him to the ship for proper care."

He was in the car seat before he'd finished speaking. He eased the car into motion again, parting the small and sympathetic crowd, and headed away on the course he'd been given.

Once in motion he said, "How's he doing?"

"He's conscious," said Lucy, "and he has a heartbeat. But I don't know whether it's right or not. I can't know what it ought to be!"

"One good thing," said Hackett. "He's getting quick action! It'll be only minutes between the crash and the hospital."

He speeded up, easing the accelerator on curves and making the best possible time without shaking his passenger. It occurred to him that he and Lucy might have done some injury in moving the alien. But he'd had to be moved away. His car had begun to burn. There'd really been no choice.

Behind them, black smoke rose skyward. The traffic went on. Hackett's car raced on its way.

Motorcycle cops did meet them. And an ambulance. But Lucy pulled her professional status and insisted that the patient not be moved until he got to the hospital. He seemed as comfortable now as his situation permitted.

So Hackett followed a motorcycle cop, with other cops and the empty ambulance trailing him. He heard Lucy talking, in the back seat. The rear-view mirror showed her leaning over the Aldarian, speaking soothingly and reassuringly, even though he could not hear her. Once she gasped.

"What's up?" demanded Hackett, not slackening speed.

"He—spoke!" said Lucy. "He said—words! Words, Jim! I don't know what they meant, but—he said words!"

They came to a town. The motorbike sirens howled.

The small fleet of cars rushed through streets. They turned into a hospital's grounds. Hackett slowed smoothly and came to a jarless stop, and then there were agitated doctors and, it seemed, crowds of nurses.

Lucy said crisply, "I'm a doctor. I think we can move him with least risk this way."

She directed the delicate job of lifting the Aldarian from the back seat onto a stretcher. She accompanied him into the hospital. Hackett pulled his car to one side and sat smoking.

A cop came over, memo pad in hand. Hackett described the accident. The cop looked Hackett's car over. No bumps. No dents.

"You didn't bump into him," he said. "What sort of guys are those Aldarians?"

Hackett said he didn't know. Reporters arrived, and vanished into the hospital. Presently two of them came out, looked around, and made for Hackett.

"Are you the man who brought that Aldarian in?" demanded one feverishly. He backed off and prepared to use a camera.

"No," said Hackett. "That man left. I brought a brother-in-law here. His wife's having triplets."

The reporters went disappointedly away. Hackett reflected sourly that they'd get his name from the police report of the accident anyway. People who knew he'd been dismissed as incompetent to learn Grek physics would be amused.

A long, long time later, there was the heavy, beating rumble of a helicopter. It settled down on a corner of the hospital grounds. Men alighted. Then two Aldarians. Then one Grek. Everybody kowtowed to the grayskinned Grek. He was a little larger than a man, he was balder than a man, and he was no longer grotesque to anybody who could see newspapers or magazine pictures or look at television. He made polite and infinitely bored gestures. He and the two Aldarians were escorted into the hospital. A little later they came out again. The two Aldarians carried a stretcher. They put it into the helicopter. The sagging rotors of the copter began to turn. They roared, and the copter rose into the air. It went away across the small town, swinging as it flew, and ultimately it vanished in the direction of that faraway place from which the Grek ship would rise on the morrow.

Again a long time later, Lucy came out of the hospital. Two male internes came with her, talking volubly. Some of their animation disappeared when she smiled brightly at Hackett. He rolled the car over to her. She climbed in and finished her conversation as she closed the door behind her.

"I'd love to see a print of those X-rays," she said sweetly. "If you think I can get them, I'll write and ask."

She waved cheerfully and Hackett drove away. They were two miles from the hospital when Lucy spoke. Then she said in a queer voice, "I did—something peculiar back there, Jim. Maybe I did wrong. I'm worried. But it happened so fast—"

"What was it?"

She hesitated. Then she said, "You were driving for the hospital after we got the Aldarian in the car. I tried to make him comfortable by straightening out his arms and legs the way I've seen them on TV. I think there are some broken bones, but of course I don't know Aldarian anatomy. He—kept moving. Stirring. I though he was in pain, and tried to help him move to the position he wanted. He watched my face. I guess they've come to recognize what our facial expressions mean. He tried desperately to make me understand something. Finally he used words. Words! How could someone whose whole race is deaf know how to form words? I kept trying to soothe him, but he kept trying to move and struggle. . . ."

Hackett's car arrived at a place where the highway he'd come on—itself a secondary road—was silhouetted against the sky. It was a solid mass of cars. They looked like an endless procession of rushing insects, black against the horizon. But then Hackett's present road turned and ran downhill and the highway traffic disappeared behind a hillside.

"I realize now," said Lucy distressedly, "he was try-

ing to make gestures. I thought he was only hurt.
Then he—tried to use words. His eyes looked desperate, but I kept on trying to soothe him. And when he
was carried into the hospital I could see that he was in
a panic. He was terrified!"

"He ought to have known that no human would
harm him," said Hackett sardonically. "At least nobody'd harm him yet. Not so long as they pass out
gifts!"

Lucy swallowed.

"I'm not at all sure I did the right thing," she said
uneasily. "When he saw the X-ray apparatus, he must
have known what it was. His eyes looked simply crazy
with despair. I bent over him, still trying to soothe
him, thinking he must know I meant well for him because we'd pulled him out of the wreck. And—somehow he touched my hand. I looked, and he was trying
to put something in it. I let him. He closed my fingers
on it, and looked at me, and his eyes—they talked,
Jim! He begged me desperately to do something about
the thing in my hand. So I—I hid it and put my finger
on my lips to say I'd keep it a secret. I don't know
how I knew he wanted me to hide it, but I did."

Hackett slowed for a traffic sign. It felt strange to
be driving on a minor road with next to no cars left,
after the bumper-to-bumper traffic he'd been in for so
long.

"You hid it," said Hackett. "On a hunch. Being a
woman, you'll call it intuition. Then what?"

"He was perfectly still while the X-rays were being
taken. He didn't look at me again. He didn't look
desperate. Then the helicopter arrived and the Grek
came in. He was very polite and somehow very lordly.
But—Greks do make you feel creepy, Jim! They do!
It's—unpleasant! Then the other two Aldarians took
the stretcher and carried the injured one out. And he
looked at me once more, just for an instant, as they
carried him away. It was—significant. He was anxious.
He was terribly anxious! But he wasn't panicky any
more. It was as if he meant that everything was all
right so far, but please don't do anything to spoil it!"

"So," said Hackett, "you kept the thing he handed you. And you kept your mouth shut, except to me. And now you suspect you should have done something else. Right?"

"Of course!" said Lucy. "I thought I'd ask you."

It is extremely likely that almost all of us, at that time, would have been shocked at the idea of anybody, for any reason, doing anything as irregular as Lucy had done. It was fortunate for the rest of us that Lucy was a woman. Only a woman would have done it.

3

THE SMALL ROAD on which Hackett drove now turned and twisted. Once it dived down and ran under a railroad crossing. For an instant the sound of the car seemed very loud, reflected as it was from the walls and ceiling of the very brief tunnel.

Then Hackett said, "He wasn't making you a gift. It wasn't an expression of gratitude for our pulling him out of the wreck and getting him to a hospital."

Lucy moistened her lips. "No. . . ."

"He didn't want the thing he gave you to show when he was X-rayed," said Hackett. "And he didn't want it given back when he went off with the Grek in the helicopter. That was pretty clear, wasn't it?"

"Y-yes," said Lucy hesitantly. "That was clear."

"He'd know the Greks would see the X-rays," observed Hackett. "He knew he'd be taken back to the ship. So it looks as if he didn't want the Greks to know about the thing he gave you. He wanted to get rid of it."

Lucy nodded. She'd reasoned the same way, after the event, but she still felt uncomfortable about what she'd done. Hackett added, "Offhand, I'm for the Aldarian. They're likeable characters. The Greks aren't. They're obviously very generous—" his tone held irony, here—"but they act too superior. And they're creepy. So I advise you to do what the Aldarian wanted you to. Keep quiet. Don't do anything. It may not be sensible, but you'll feel better if you do."

Lucy said, relieved, "I was going to anyway, but I'm glad you agree."

"In confidence," said Hackett, "I have a reason."

"What? And don't you want to look at the thing?"

"Not now," said Hackett. "I think I want to keep moving. And I wish I hadn't given our names to that cop!"

He drove on. There was bright sunshine, and little white cumulus clouds seeming like islands floating upon the ocean of the sky. Hackett had felt definitely sour for a good part of the time the Grek ship had been aground. It was a vessel of a civilization so far advanced that we humans were savages by comparison. Its officers behaved with a sort of aloof politeness that some people took for cordiality, but there was boredom behind it.

The Greks were not interested in man's achievements. They weren't interested in human beings as persons. They gave, indifferently, the information that should turn Earth into a terrestrial paradise when understood and applied. But they showed no enjoyment in their benevolence. They acted like men who didn't care for children, who gave toys or candy to them without feeling pleasure in the action. There was something wrong; something lacking.

And we who were right there saw it and didn't understand what it was!

Hackett made what time he could. He didn't try to get back even to a secondary road. They were too crowded. He stayed on the back roads, the service roads, the third-rate highways between small towns and villages. But they were chosen to lead gradually to the place from which the Grek ship would presently rise and disappear.

Oddly enough, by taking those back roads Hackett made better speed than most drivers. He arrived at the Grek ship's cradle after sundown, but hours earlier than some travelers on the jammed main roads. He arrived, in fact, early enough to be able to reserve a sleeping cubbyhole for Lucy for overnight. He could only get one, so he would have to sleep in his car. But he didn't mind.

When that arrangement was complete, they were hungry. Miles of land had been devoted to preparations for the lift-off ceremony. There were incredibly vast parking areas, already partly filled. The gigantic stands for onlookers covered acres upon acres. The bunting-draped auditorium was large enough even for the intended departure ball.

And naturally, in such a setting and for such a purpose, there were many minor enterprises designed to make a fast dollar. Hackett and Lucy got something to eat. There was no restaurant—because this event would last only twenty-four hours or so—but for hamburgers of inferior quality and uniced soft drinks he paid the price of a six-course dinner at an expensive nightclub. For the cubbyhole reserved for Lucy, he paid the price of a Presidential suite in a metropolitan hotel.

He and Lucy peered into the huge canvas-roofed hall where the predeparture ball would be held. It was abundantly draped with colored bunting which was too cheap to be opaque. The unpainted framing of the walls showed through. The floor had been hastily laid. There was the smell of sawdust. High up around the walls were the projection-TV screens to link all the celebrations, everywhere, into one.

"They say," said Hackett in a dry voice, "that there'll be ten thousand couples dancing here tonight. In honor of the Greks, of course. A highly suitable event. I'm sure they'll be lost in admiration!"

Lucy nodded. They went outside and found themselves passing a gate and entering the now silent, roofless, enormous grandstands. If they'd been built in any but the most penny-pinching manner, they would have been a remarkable spectacle in themselves. They completely surrounded the quarter-mile-long Grek ship.

Hackett and Lucy saw the ship, now.

It was wholly past belief. Partly buried in the cradle

dug out for it to rest in, it was still more huge than
any manmade object on Earth. It was five city blocks
long, and though its cradle had been dug out to a depth
of more than a hundred feet, its rounded upper surface,
glittering in the moonlight, reached as high as the roof
of a fifty-story building. It was overwhelming in its
massiveness. It was daunting because of sheer size.
There were men working on a platform before its
forward end, installing microphones and cameras on a
platform for the departure broadcast. They looked
smaller than ants. The glaring lights they worked by
were pinpoints of brightness in the black shadow cast
by the ship in the moonlight.

"I don't think," said Hackett detachedly, "that anything as big as that can be imagined to be benevolent.
The most plausible thing one can believe is that it's
indifferent."

He moved purposefully along one of the walkways of
the grandstand. Lucy followed, shivering a little. Greks
were not much larger than men. Aldarians were not as
tall as the average human. To think of such relative
mites controlling anything so gigantic appalled her.
And her imagination refused to picture them as con-
structing such a ship.

There was another matter. The Greks had let it be
inferred that there were no more than six or seven—at
most a dozen—Grek officers and instructors aboard.
They had definitely said the class of student Aldarians
was limited to forty or fifty members. So small a ship's
company in so vast a ship seemed unreasonable. But
pure frustration followed an effort to conceive what
the rest of the ship contained.

Humans had been aboard, to be sure, but not one
had gone beyond a single passageway and two or three
small compartments at its end. No man knew more of
the inside of the ship than that. The Greks ignored hints
for a larger view. And they were so lavish with information by which the world should profit, that nobody wanted to offend them by impertinent curiosity.

As he went along the walkway, Hackett glanced
again at the monstrosity of shining metal. It had not

stirred since its arrival. It had displayed no weapon. It remained a mystery. Neither Greks—on the rare occasions when one or more of them left it—nor Aldarians had given any information about it. The Greks did explain that its space drive could only be understood and used by engineers fully understanding the scientific principles they were now trying to teach to carefully selected human students. But they'd rated Hackett as incapable of that training.

"They've announced," said Hackett detachedly, "that some of their Aldarian crewmen have volunteered to stay on Earth and help us get started toward civilization. Remarkable altruism! The Greks say they don't expect to be back in this part of the galaxy for a good ten of our years, and they say the trip isn't worth while for a single uncivilized world's commerce. But another training ship will be ordered to stop by and pick up the Aldarian volunteers eventually."

Lucy looked at him curiously. "I didn't know that."

"It will be in the newspapers tomorrow," he said sardonically. "There's been some fear that we're too stupid to carry on with only what information they've given us so far. The theory of the power-broadcast system still hasn't fully been grasped by any of us natives. If we're to develop past the elementary stuff they're leaving with us, we have to have more instruction. Several governments asked for it. So there'll be some Aldarians staying here."

He turned again, this time down steps toward the grandstands' central space, in which the Grek ship lay motionless. Again Lucy followed.

She said suddenly, "Are you going somewhere special, Jim?"

He nodded and went on. He turned to the right, and saw signs. This was section such-and-such, sub-section such-and-such, and aisle so-and-so. He came to a gate, held it wide. It opened upon a flight of steps going down under the rows of plank grandstand seats. He offered Lucy his hand for security and they went down and down and down. Streaks of star-studded sky could be seen between the seat planks overhead. There

were struts and braces everywhere to support the
weight of the crowd the stands would hold on the
morrow.

There were small tarpapered temporary structures
on the ground. Light showed out of the windows. They
reached the bottom of the steps. Here were four or
five roughly built one-story shacks.

"Emergency stuff," said Hackett explanatorily.
"First-aid stations. Bulldozer shelters. We're going to
the one yonder—the smallest one. You've got the thing
the Aldarian gave you?"

"Of course," said Lucy uneasily.

"I advise you to turn it over to the people I'll intro-
duce you to," said Hackett. "But that's your decision.
If you feel like mentioning it after you know them, do
so. Otherwise don't."

They went forward, past the first of the jerrybuilt
structures. Inside it, someone was talking over the
telephone. The second building was long and high. It
had enormous doors so the earth-moving machinery
could get in. The next building was a first-aid station.
Lighted windows allowed a glimpse of hospital beds
inside. In the last shack there was a television set
turned on. Hackett opened the door without knocking
and ushered Lucy in.

It was brightly lighted, with three unshaded electric
bulbs, and there were four men in it. Three of them
were barely Hackett's age, and there was one man with
gold-rimmed spectacles and startling wisps of sandy-
colored hair. Two of the younger ones played cards.
The third leaned back in his chair with his hands
behind his head, blowing smoke rings at the ceiling.
Those three looked as if they might be graduate students, or maybe college seniors. The man with sandy
hair seemed to be listening critically to strange, supposedly musical sounds from the television set. He
looked up, nodded, and rose. Hackett introduced them
in turn.

"This is the Rogers University strictly unofficial
archaeological expedition to the Grek ship's lift-off,"
he explained to Lucy. "They're here because they're

the only people who thought I might be worth listening to, after the Greks rated me as a retarded child."

The man with the wispy hair had been introduced as Clark. He grinned.

"We diggers are classed subnormal, too," he said comfortably. "So we think kindly of Jim. He was on the Rogers faculty, you know. We've got better than an even chance of finding out some interesting stuff here. It wouldn't have been thought of except for Jim."

The younger man who'd been smoking said judicially, "It's a most promising idea. If it works out we may rise in status from archaeologists to garbage analysts. A new profession, and a distinguished one!"

Lucy said helplessly, "I don't quite understand."

"Tell her," suggested Hackett.

"We're going to analyze the Grek garbage," said Clark cheerfully. "It's Jim's idea. When the Army dug out a cradle for the ship to land in, they naturally planted a few atom bombs under it—to have in the house in case of sickness, you might say. They also planted underground microphones to find out if the Greks detected them and dug them out. They didn't. The atomic boys are tearing their hair right now; but their ground microphones *did* report that, though the Greks didn't bother the bombs, they did dig a hole somewhere else. From time to time they've dumped stuff in it. The obvious conclusion is garbage. So we're going to examine it after they leave."

"And we're experienced," said another of the younger men. "We can tell plenty from a garbage pit a thousand years old. There's no telling what we can do with fresher material."

The third of the younger men added mildly, "One archaeologist found out and proved that the average sandal size of Roman legionaries was almost exactly the same as the modern child's size-ten shoe. You see? We may do wonders!"

The television set broke off its musical broadcast. A "Special Bulletin" line appeared on its screen. A voice said resonantly, "At the request of the commanding officer of the Grek ship, we offer this special bulletin. Early today an Aldarian member of the Grek ship's crew was badly injured in an automobile accident on his way to rejoin his ship. His injuries would have caused his death but for the prompt action of a Mr. James Hackett and a Doctor Lucy Thale, who rushed him to a human hospital, communicated with the Grek ship, and thereby saved his life. The Grek commander wishes to express his gratitude to these two persons. Will they get in touch with him? All human authorities have been asked to bring them to the Grek ship immediately, to receive evidence of the gratitude the Greks wish to express."

The "Special Bulletin" line disappeared. After a moment's pause the musical din resumed.

Hackett looked grimly at Lucy. She was pale. He said, "No! Absolutely not!"

She shook her head.

"I'd—much rather not. I was near that Grek in the hospital. I felt—I felt horribly creepy! I don't want to go near any of them again!"

"And I won't let you," said Hackett flatly.

"If you won't go, I won't," said Lucy shakily. "So that's settled. But do you think they can find us?"

The sandy-haired Clark looked shrewdly from one to the other.

"We don't want to be found," Hackett told him coldly. "Lucy'll tell you why—if she wants to."

Carefully, hesitatingly, Lucy told the story of the Aldarian's wreck, his attempt to tell her something, and his desperately forming words, when all Aldarians were supposed to be congenitally deaf. If they were a race that had never heard sounds, they couldn't possibly have developed a spoken language. But—

She stopped and looked at Hackett. He made no sign to tell her either to end it there or to go on. She had to make the decision. So she hesitated for a moment, and then described the terrified effort of the injured alien to thrust something into her hand, and the impassioned pleading that she hide it.

Clark said briskly, "Hm. The Grek who came for him didn't think of thanking you then, did he? It seems odd that he'd develop an urgent gratitude only after some time and a possible—ah—discovery that there was something going on he didn't approve of. Did you keep what was given you?"

She produced it. It was a small, flat, round object, hardly larger than a woman's wrist watch. There was a stud on one side which could be moved. The flat part of one surface yielded a little to pressure. The object wasn't finely finished. Tool marks remained on it. It wasn't a timepiece. It wasn't anything that could be imagined. It was wholly cryptic.

The sandy-haired man examined it very carefully. He did not shift the stud in any way. He said meditatively, "In our line, we don't go pushing things around at random. They might break. I'd be inclined to X-ray this very carefully to see what's inside. This isn't a Grek artifact, you know! There's a feel to such things. I've seen Grek objects. This is not one. Considering everything, I'd say it was definitely Aldarian."

"I don't know what to do with it," said Lucy.

"I'll find out," said Clark, "with your permission." She nodded, and he put the object in a small safe. He explained, "We de..'t know what we may find, so we have this safe here to keep souvenir hunters from making off with anything we do find." Then he added, "This is no time or place to play with your gift. We don't know what it may do."

There was a tap on the door. He spun the safe's knob while one of the younger men got up and opened the door. A policeman came in.

"Sorry to bother you," he said amiably, "but you people come from Rogers University, don't you?"

"That's right," said Clark, cordially. "What's up?"

"Nothing bad," the policeman assured him. "There was a guy named Hackett who used to be there. You know him?"

"Yes," said Clark. "Physics Department. What about him?"

"He did the Greks a big favor," explained the uniformed man. "They want to find him and a girl who was in the car with him. Want to give him a present or something. They're anxious about it. So they asked us to hunt up everybody he might get in touch with and have 'em tell him."

"Right," said Clark. "If I see him, I'll tell him. He'll report in at traffic headquarters."

"Fine! If he comes there they'll tell the Greks he's turned up. He and that girl are kind of heroic, to the Greks. They want to do something for 'em. I wouldn't mind being in his shoes, would you?"

"Not a bit," said Clark. "If I see him I'll certainly tell him."

The policeman went out. There was silence. After a moment Hackett said, "Thanks." Then he added, "I gave my name and Lucy's to the cop who wanted to report the accident. I also gave my car license number. And Lucy's registered by name for one of those cubbyholes with a bunk in it. If the Greks have gone as far as having the police look up people who might know me, the cops will have my car and Lucy's bunk staked out. With the best of intentions, of course!"

The man with wispy hair nodded. Then he said to Lucy, "Don't worry. You brought us something we want to look at. If the Greks overwhelmed you with presents and then asked about it. . . . But I can't figure why their gratitude's so great only after so long an interval. Anyhow, we're your confederates in whatever you've done. We won't tell on you!"

Lucy tried to smile, but she was extremely uneasy.

"Mysterious characters, the Greks," said Clark. "They've got the atomic boys tearing their hair. They have some bombs planted under the ship. Naturally, they made arrangements for testing the firing circuits. And they did, even after the Greks began to act benevolent. That's mysterious, when you think of it! Why are they so kind to us? Anyhow, the firing circuits don't work. The bombs couldn't be set off if somebody wanted to. The Greks have done something to them without bothering to dig them up. The atomic people don't like that."

He turned down the music from the television set. It had seemed to Hackett rather worse than the average noises of that kind. But perhaps this was especially in honor of the Greks, too.

"I'm not too confident," said Clark, worriedly. "They're smart! They might have garbage-disposal units that will spoil their wastes as a source of information. And it'll be too late to picket the ship with signs saying, 'Greks are Unfair to Garbage Analysts.' "

He smiled and said reassuringly to Lucy, "But don't worry. We're going to look for information the Greks don't want us to have. Which is ingratitude, but very much like us humans. Are you two going to the ball?"

Hackett shook his head. He was deeply uneasy. His pride had been hurt by the Greks' disqualification of him for instruction in their science. He didn't believe in Grek science, yet there was something about it which mystified everybody who tried to grasp it. Now he was baffled and made acutely uneasy by the sudden excessive gratitude of the Greks for an action which —as Lucy verified—had not caused a glance or a gesture of appreciation in the hospital.

Time went on. The television music went off. There was a commercial, especially designed as a tribute to the Greks, about to leave Earth enriched behind them. It promised that when better power receivers were made, so-and-so would make them. Meanwhile it urged listeners to wait until the receivers could be put on the market. There was more sponsored entertainment, adulating the Greks.

An hour after the first special bulletin, the line appeared on the screen again. There was a second announcement of the ardent desire of the Greks to reward Hackett and Lucy for their kindness to an injured crewman. Behind the announcer's voice there were resonant sounds. Voices. Footsteps. A musical instrument hooted briefly. The farewell party for the Greks was about to begin.

"I think," said Hackett, "that if I could get Lucy a couple of thousand miles away tonight, I'd do it. Since I can't, I want to keep her and myself out of sight until the Greks are gone. I don't know why."

"Be our guests," said Clark cheerfully. "We aren't

advertising our intentions. The Greks might not like them. We're co-conspirators. Be our guests."

Hackett was disturbed. He couldn't fully account to himself for his point of view about this affair. Now, of course, we can see why he should have thought this way. It wasn't reasonable for a highly advanced race like the Greks to take the trouble they'd done for a backward and practically uncivilized world like ours. There could be no possible way for us to return their kindness. It wasn't even sensible of them to be so generous, so it was foolish for us to believe in their overwhelming benevolence.

But we did. We did! We were the prize imbeciles of the galaxy.

4

THERE WERE farewell parties all over Earth that night. The departure time for the Grek ship had been arranged so the maximum number of television receivers could show the spectacle live. That meant, naturally, that it should occur during daylight on the western hemisphere. So it was scheduled for noon by Eastern Standard Time, in the United States. People on the west coast wouldn't have to get up too early to watch the more-than-historical event, and people in western Europe wouldn't have gone to bed. The rest of the world would see the show taped and edited twelve hours later.

But the farewell parties were something else. They varied with the longitude of the place where they occurred.

Not all of them were carried even in part on the satellite-relay news coverage system. In India they tended to be uninhibited. In Africa they were hypnotic, rythmic, and emotional. There was a Greek party which was almost frigidly intellectual, and in Germany it was said that more beer was drunk in less time by more people than ever before joined in a single celebration. The British parties featured a wire-carried address by the prime minister (with political overtones), and the French festivities caused a cabinet crisis on the morning after, though the party itself was a social success. The Russians staged a parade through Red Square, with torches making a magnificent picture. The Scandinavian parties were gargantuan banquets, the Austrialian ones featured athletes of national stature, and in the United States—

The parties reflected the national mores. There was no motion picture or television star unoccupied on the night of the farewell for the Greks. There were few outstanding politicians who didn't manage to appear on some broadcast at some time, someplace. There were great wingdings held wherever space could be found for more than a thousand couples to dance. There were overflow parties at smaller dancing places, and the number of private celebrations was never even guessed at.

The party at the departure site, though, was stupendous. Everybody was celebrating in an all-pervading emotional binge the fact that everybody was now a millionaire, or would be as soon as a few formalities were done with. It was settled; it was certain; it was fixed in the pattern of the future that as soon as things became a little more organized, nobody would work more than one day a week, nobody would work at all after forty, and everybody would have everything that anybody else had.

There was so far no very clear idea of what people would do with their new leisure, and nobody seemed to wonder about the consequences of being deprived of all objects for ambition. Each person seemed to feel as if he'd inherited at least a million dollars, which would be paid him next week or, at the latest, the week after. The prospect required celebration.

So the party at the departure site was a brawl from the beginning.

Down in the small shed under the grandstand, Hackett watched the television screen from beneath frowning brows. The vast plank dance floor was hardly

visible because of the people on it. The music for
dancing was nearly inaudible, because of the clamor
of voices and the scrape of feet upon the wooden floor.
The sound was a babbling through which, at intervals,
the boom of a bass horn made its way, and rather more
often the disconnected and bizarre notes of a trumpet.

The television camera angle changed. It showed a
TV star signing autographs. It changed again. There
was a drunk—this early in the evening—trying to do
a particularly fancy dance. There was a clear space
around him. Back to a long shot with a wide-angle lens,
showing thousands upon thousands of people moving
more or less in rhythm, but certainly not hearing the
music, certainly not mingling, yet somehow convinced
that they were having a good time.

"I don't think we're missing anything," said Hackett,
"by not being there."

Lucy nodded, but she was inattentive. She seemed
to be listening to other sounds.

"There," said the sandy-haired Clark, sadly, "there
is the basic problem of the human race. We'll adjust
to it eventually, and maybe it will be worth the price
we pay. But I wonder!"

Lucy moistened her lips. She couldn't pay attention.
One of the younger men went out of the shack. She
strained her ears as she heard him move about outside.

"People should listen to us archaeologists more,"
said Clark. He didn't seem to care whether anyone
listened or not. "In the old days—five hundred to fifty
thousand years back—things changed slowly. King-
doms fell and civilizations died, but never in a rush.
Those things happened because climates changed and
people had to move, and fight for a place to move to.
But those things didn't happen overnight. Things are
different nowadays.

"When my grandfather was a boy, men fastened
clean stiff collars and cuffs to their shirts so they
could wear the body of the shirt for a full week.
Women canned vegetables for winter. They swept with
brooms, washed in tubs, and made their own soap.

Then, suddenly, they got vacuum cleaners and detergents and preserved foods and washing machines and dishwashers. Things changed fast! And what did we people do? What did women do with all their new leisure? With the time they didn't have to spend sweeping and washing and canning and making soap? You know what they did! They raised their standards of what was clean and how their families should be fed and how often they should take a bath. They cancelled out their spare time! They raised their sights; they aimed higher, to keep from having leisure!

"The same with men. There was a time when a man with a flint hoe might cultivate a garden the size of a city lot. Then he got better tools. He got livestock. But did he keep to the same size garden and enjoy the leisure he could have? Hell, no! He started to farm acres. Tens of acres. Then hundreds! We humans can't take leisure. We simply can't take it!"

He grinned around the strictly temporary shack, which smelled of sawdust and unpainted wood.

"And now," he asked of the floors and walls, "now what will we do? Our way of life has to change, and practically overnight. If what the Greks have given us makes us need to work only one day a week, and not at all for three-quarters of our lives, what'll we do? The one thing certain is that we won't loaf! That's the curse of Adam, that we have to work whether we need to or not. We *have* to. What new set of demands will we make of ourselves to cancel out leisure such as the Greks are thrusting on us?"

Hackett shrugged, still watching the television screen.

There were footsteps outside. Lucy tensed. But it was the young man who'd gone out a few minutes before. He came in and said, "The Greks are entertaining. I just saw a man come out of the ship. He's a big shot, to judge by his medals. A foreigner. As soon as he was out, another man went in. He wore a diplomatic uniform too."

"The Greks are giving audiences," said Clark, "to

prominent citizens. Representatives of the big nations. Why?"

There was no answer. The television screen showed a very famous comedy star making a speech to the celebrators. Not all that he said could be heard, but he cracked jokes, orated humorously about the wonderful time everybody was having, and then made a practiced transition to a pathetic-patriotic bit, spouted for the Greks whom all delighted to honor. When he was done, the camera shot changed and a voice announced that through satellite relay there would be a series of scenes from other farewell parties around the world.

They were only selections, of course. There were too many parties for even half to be transmitted over oceans. Those that were shown were dull. New Delhi. Alexandria. Berlin. Paris. Stockholm. Mexico City. Edinburgh.

A light began to flick off and on in the corner where equipment for archaeological research was stacked. One of the three young men called out. Clark snapped off the television. Someone adjusted something, listening painstakingly.

There came thumphing sounds. The four men in the archaeological party listened with strained attention. There was a metallic clank and then more cushioned bumping sounds. To Hackett it sounded like things being thrown into a hole.

Clark said swiftly, "Underground microphone listening under the Grek ship. It sounds as if they're filling up their garbage pit before leaving. The Army let me hear a tape of the same kind of noises. They've picked it up several times."

They continued to listen. The atmosphere in the little shack was very peculiar. Rough planking formed the walls of the single room. The floor was unfinished, but in one corner there was a pile of equipment for cryptic uses. One of the younger archaeologists hung over a particular instrument, from which indefinite sounds came at erratic intervals.

Hackett saw Lucy's expression, and moved a chair

to where she could sit comfortably. The noises went on. There were more clanking sounds, and presently the irregular and intermittent noises ceased and a steady thumping took its place.

"They're finished with the garbage," said Clark. "They're putting in a top fill of dirt, and tamping it. Tidying up before they go away."

The thumping sounds continued for a time; then they stopped. The strained attention of the occupants of the shack lessened. Clark looked pleased. "We'll have something to dig up; that's certain!"

One of the younger archaeologists said, "Five gets you ten there's stuff in there from halfway around the world."

Clark spread out his hands. He wouldn't bet. Hackett asked, "Why? Did they ask for samples of stuff?"

"It's an argument," said the one who'd offered the bet. "Nobody's sure, but there've been Johnson detector reports from different places. Some people say the Greks have a flying something—nobody's seen it—and that they've made some exploration flights."

"But radar—"

"We've tried to make things radar-black, so they'll absorb radar frequencies and not reflect any of them. We haven't succeeded too well, though the Greks may have. But a Johnson detector would spot a flying thing because it wasn't the same temperature as the sky. That's what's been reported. In a heavy rain, though, or even through clouds, a Johnson detector isn't all one could wish. If they picked storms to take off and return in, we couldn't be sure. Maybe that's what they've done."

Hackett said, "But there's been no hint of such a thing in the news."

"Naturally," said Clark blandly. "The Greks are our friends. In a way, they're our Santa Clauses. Who'd suspect Santa Claus of anything wrong? Why, the bombs under their ship can't be set off!"

Then his tone changed. "Actually, nobody's sure. And in strict honesty, the bombs and the microphones were planted before we were certain they meant us no harm. What's been done in the way of radar watch and so on—including the Johnson detector stuff—was practically routine. We humans like to find out things. The Greks told us plenty, but we wanted to find out more. It's curiosity, not necessarily suspicion."

He moved to turn the television set on again.

"Anyhow, to most people news is purely entertainment. They know what they want to hear. They tune out everything else. So the networks don't broadcast anything that would offend anybody. And anything suggesting bad faith by the Greks—That would be too frightening! The great, democratic, enlightened public would raise the devil!"

He turned the switch. The television screen lighted again. There was a "Special Bulletin" line on it. A voice said: ". . . Hackett and a Doctor Lucy Thale, who rushed him to a human hospital, communicated with the Grek ship, and thereby saved his life. The Grek commander wishes to express his gratitude to these two persons. Will they get in touch with the commander through any human authority? All human officials have been asked to bring them to the Grek ship to receive evidences of the gratitude the Greks wish to express."

The "Special Bulletin" line vanished. The farewell party came back. It was essentially unchanged. The floor was practically invisible because of the crowd which believed it was dancing. There were some areas, though, where people had given up the attempt to hear the music and merely walked about or talked, assuring themselves and each other that they were enjoying themselves hugely. And there were more drunks.

Hackett said deliberately, "You're very careful not to express any suspicion of the Greks. I've tried not to feel any, but I do. It occurs to me that they're making a very timely flit. They've been aground for six months. They've done marvelous things for us, yes. But the side effects of those marvelous things are beginning to show up. If the Greks stayed on, they'd be blamed for them. If they go away, their departure will seem the cause of any troubles we may have."

The sandy-haired man nodded. "You mean unemployment?"

Hackett said angrily, "Worldwide, it's now twenty per cent, and getting worse. Factories have to shut down to retool for the products we want because we couldn't make them before. But nobody's making the products we need right along. Only one car in eight is a Grek designed broadcast-power job, but no more gasoline cars are being turned out. That's raising the number of people on unemployment. The bottom has dropped out of all fuel industries, though there aren't enough broadcast-power receivers to keep things going. The crops look as if they'll be so big—"

He stopped. People came along the walkway outside, having descended the stairs from the grandstands. They came in, several men and two women. One of the women was Clark's wife. The other was a young girl. They already looked exhausted. Clark's wife exclaimed at the sight of Hackett, and her husband said, "I know! I know! He's been paged. But it's all taken care of. Only he doesn't want reporters hounding him for a human-interest story on how it feels to rescue an Aldarian. How's the party?"

"Horrible!"

The opinion was unanimous. The newcomers sat down and described the party. It could be seen better on television, and anything was preferable to actually being there. Hackett hardly listened. He watched Lucy. She seemed panic-stricken.

He told her, "You're supposedly wanted for praise and presents, so nobody'll tell on you. If the Greks called you a criminal, it might be another matter; but nobody'll turn you in to be praised."

It was true. Gradually her apprehension lessened. The television showed scenes from the Rio de Janeiro farewell party. From Amsterdam. The Pacific Coast party. That broadcast fairly dripped publicity plugs for motion pictures or television series, mentioned by the picture people who crowded common citizens off the camera.

Hackett heard somebody saying, "It's really weird!

I saw one of the texts. Of course the Greks' idea of grammar is out of this world, but the book starts off lucidly, and gradually it begins to get fuzzy, and then tricky, and all of a sudden you're reading pure gibberish. And in your own line, too!"

It was one of the men who'd come down from the party, talking about a Grek scientific treatise. Hackett reflected that other people had the same trouble understanding the Greks.

Minutes later someone else was saying, "It's fantastic! The worst unemployment situation in history, and people who do have jobs are staying home, because soon they won't have to work more than eight hours a week."

The television announced a speech by a frequent Presidential candidate. Its climax was the introduction of the commander of the Grek ship. He was larger than a man, and he sat in a chair that was very intricately worked. His skin was a moderately light gray and singularly inflexible, as if composed of smooth plates. He bent his head in recognition of the literally deafening applause and cheering his appearance evoked.

He waited it out without expression. Then, when miniature human figures appeared before his image, waving and gesticulating for silence, he touched a small button on the side of his chair.

"He's on the ship!" said someone in astonishment. "They're rebroadcasting a projection, and he's on the ship!"

Someone else said, "He's at a good many thousands of parties. Listen!"

A human voice spoke. It changed. Another voice spoke. The effect was bewildering. But the way the Greks communicated with humans had been explained often enough. Their original breakthrough to human speech had been the rebroadcast of six human words from all the tens of thousands that had been beamed at the ship when it was alongside the moon. Then the Greks had required no more than two days to acquire a vocabulary of recorded human voices speaking individual words. They combined those words into phrases and sentences. The speech of the Grek commander to the people of Earth was an aggregation of some thousands of words spoken at different times by hundreds of human voices. It was not recorded in any ordinary sense. It was assembled from recordings.

The effect was without inflection or expression. It sounded inhuman. It even sounded creepy.

The gray-skinned, impassive figure of the Grek commander—if it were the Grek commander—sat motionless while his message to the people of Earth was delivered in their voices for them to hear.

The speech ended. The screen in the tarpaper shack went blank, as did the giant projection screens at the departure site party and all the other screens of all sizes and sorts all over the Earth. Then ardently enthusiastic figures leaped up to act as cheerleaders of the screaming uproar arising in honor of the Grek.

The parties, after that, were essentially anticlimatic. The television screens stayed alight and professionally interesting commentators poured out thousands of words of description and background. But the life had gone out of the parties after the Grek commander vanished.

Clark's wife announced firmly that she was not going back to that outrageous cubbyhole to sleep. There was no ventilation! She would sleep here, in a chair. The young girl agreed with her. It seemed perfectly reasonable for Lucy to make the same decision.

Hackett went outside with the other men, to smoke. Long narrow stripes of moonlight came down between the seat planks of the grandstand. Braces and beams and stiffening struts formed a peculiar ceiling to the space below them.

A figure in uniform came over from the bulldozer shed. It was the Army officer in charge of the earth-moving machinery. Clark told him of the underground noise indicating that a Grek garbage pit had been filled and tamped down. The officer nodded. He wasn't surprised.

There was nothing in particular to be done. They talked desultorily, waiting for sunrise. When that came, they'd wait for lift-off time. After that, they'd wait for the crowds to leave. Then the bulldozers would dig up the atom bombs and try to find out what had happened to their firing mechanisms so that on test they reported dead. The bombs couldn't be exploded.

But Hackett found himself very much inclined to jitter. He wanted the Greks gone from Earth. So did the Army officer. So did the unofficial Rogers University archaeological expedition. The Greks had given humanity the equivalent of centuries of painstaking research and development. They were leaving Earth while human gratitude was at its peak. Everybody expected that from now on—or as soon as things were organized—nobody would have to do anything to justify his existence. It seemed an infinitely alluring prospect to most people. Hackett said so, sourly.

"But personally," he added with distaste, "what bothers me is that I apparently won't be allowed to justify my existence."

The Army officer made a scornful noise. "For real frustration," he said bitterly, "you might try how it feels to know that all you've trained for and built your life on is about as useful as a hole in the head."

He spoke savagely of the Greks' having made the military capable of nothing but the production of disaster, instead of the defense of their country, or even their race.

"It looks to me," said Hackett, "as if a lot of us are ungrateful for what most of our fellow humans most desire."

He found that it was possible to view the state of things dispassionately now. It was true that not everybody would want the benefits the Greks had made possible. Knowing oneself to be inferior and primitive and at the mercy of aliens whose presence produced a feeling of creepy dread and horror—that was a high price. To some people it would seem too much to pay for progress.

They smoked, and talked fragmentarily and to no purpose. The slatlike streaks of moonlight moved across the ground under the grandstands. At very,

very long last the sky grayed to the east, and in due time the sun rose.

One of the archaeological party went off to buy coffee. The Army officer disappeared among his bull-dozers. There were vague stirrings here and there.

The coffee was very bad, with the sole virtue of being hot. It was flavored by the paper containers in which it came. Hackett paced restlessly. He'd found that other people shared some of his doubts about the Greks, but there was nothing definite to blame on them. Displayed weapons or no displayed weapons, humanity was helpless against the Greks. It was neces-sary to believe in their benevolence, or one would grow mad with fear. But after all, there was no evidence against their kindliness. The Aldarians were lively, friendly, cordial creatures. They got along with the Greks. The Greks had given us so many things. . . .

The people who presently began to fill the stands appeared to have no doubts whatever. Some had come to cheer the departing Greks. Some tended to sniffle sentimentally at the departure of those who had done so much for mankind. There were people who were already maudlin about the benefits that needed just a little more organization to become available to every-body. . . .

Those of us who sat in the stands that morning re-member the atmosphere. Some of us have trouble believing that we actually shed tears of gratitude while the interminable program went on. Tears of boredom would probably have been more sensible.

It was an appalling performance. There were school-children marching to give bouquets to the Greks—or, rather, to the solitary Grek who sat through what must have been unutterable tedium for him. There was a prominent artist who presented a painted portrait of one of the ship's officers. There were representatives of industry who presented special examples of their manufactures, either made of gold or thriftily gold plated, for the Greks to remember them by. The motion picture industry presented a gold-plated movie projector with twenty gold-plated cans of news film

portraying Greks and Aldarians in full color on their
rare excursions from their ship. There were scrolls of
fulsome praise extending honorary membership in
hereditary societies. Fraternal orders presented certifi-
cates of special qualification, plus the regalia for the
celebration of mysterious rites wherever the Greks
came from or went back to.

Such events were at least varied. But the speeches.
. . .

Every politician on Earth tried to be allowed to
say a few appropriate words. When speech-making
was restricted to prime ministers or heads of state of
nations in being, the time required was still impossibly
long. Sternly ordered to restrict their speeches to four
minutes each, they appeared in hordes, and none spoke
under six minutes. Several had to be hauled without
dignity away from the microphones.

At long last the business was done. It was noon,
Eastern Standard Time. The lone Grek who had
endured all this mishmash stood up. With complete
impassiveness he walked across the wooden walk from
the speaker's platform to the ship. He went into it.
The entry port closed. Men hastily pulled the walkway
aside. For a while nobody noticed that the departure
presents still stayed where they'd been set down. Some
of the watchers might have expected to see this over-
sight repaired, but nothing happened. From bouquets
to gold-plated cans of film, they stayed where they'd
been placed. And then, without fanfare of any sort, the
ship lifted, silently and steadily and with no ceremony
at all.

The crowds in the stands burst into cheers. The
unnumbered thousands who'd been unable to get
tickets for the stands, cheered from the spaces beyond
them. The Grek ship rose and rose, with a chorus of
grateful human voices following it. Presently its huge-
ness was no longer oppressive. Soon it was only a
sliver of glittering metal rising ever more swiftly toward the heavens. And after a while it could not be
seen at all.

The Greks had gone away, as they said they intended

to, leaving a dozen Aldarians to help us become civilized. And we began to face certain unease-producing facts. We'd been left alone to fumble at the situation the Greks had left. They said they'd go, and they visibly had. They said they were heading back to their home star cluster, and we had no reason to doubt them. They said some Grek ship would stop by to pick up the Aldarian volunteers in ten of our years or so. They said we couldn't expect to see them back in less time than that.

We believed them, and we were uneasy because we believed them! Heaven help us, we—were—uneasy—because—we—believed—them!

Maybe, though, we'd have done worse if suspicion of the truth had become widespread. When things began to be found out, nobody in authority dared to make them public. Which, it can be said, some students of the matter consider to be the only intelligent decision made by anybody of importance—except those who came to work secretly with Hackett.

5

"I'D FEEL BETTER," said Hackett, "if I could decide whether the Greks were displaying indifference or contempt in that lift-off performance of theirs."

He and Lucy and the others of the tarpaper-shack archaeological group were watching the crowds trying to leave the scene of the Greks' departure. It was an astonishing spectacle. There was a large space in which buses had parked after bringing their loads of onlookers to the lift-off site. The buses were now surrounded by confused groups of people who, having waited through one of the most tedious ceremonies ever conceived by the mind of man, were impatient at the least delay in beginning the almost equally tedious journeys back to where they'd come from.

There were private cars trying helplessly to get through the mobs of people, then trying to get to their cars so they could try helplessly to get through other mobs trying to get to their cars. The attempt at leaving, of course, began at the parts of the parking fields nearest the grandstands, because those car owners reached their vehicles first. It was an arrangement designed for the maximum of confusion.

It seemed that hours passed before even the buses were filled, and the people who had become separated from their traveling companions who had their bus tickets either found them or gathered near information booths set up for the purpose. Traffic police borrowed from six neighboring states began to get things moving, through inexplicable and irrational stoppages still frustrated them. Lost children contributed to the uproar, while the parents they'd lost increased the tumult. Inevitably, anybody who got to his car immediately started its motor while waiting for a chance to move, and a fog of mephitic fuel fumes spread for miles. Only the Grek-designed cars did not burn gasoline, and contributed nothing to the unwholesomeness.

It was quite a spectacle. Underneath the grandstand, where Hackett and Lucy watched, there was a sort of echoing stillness. The ground was littered with crumpled paper candy wrappers, popcorn containers, chewing-gum packages and cigarette butts to mark where human crowds had been. Outside, swirling dust arose to mingle with gasoline fumes and the confused murmur of the mob.

"They figured," said Clark, "that there'd be a million and a half people here. I think they guessed wrong. That's too low."

The Army officer from the bulldozer sheds said sourly to Hackett, "Indifference or contempt? How do you mean that?"

"What do they think of us?" asked Hackett. "They've given us all sorts of things we need, but they haven't bothered to be pleasant about it, only polite. That could be indifference. On the other hand, the elaborate gifts we got ready for them, they didn't bother to carry away. And that could be contempt."

The Army officer considered. After a moment he

said with some grimness, "I hope it's indifference. I wouldn't mind not getting to know them better. But contempt—"

"I don't think it's contempt," protested Lucy. "They went to a lot of trouble to do us good, to give us things we need and haven't had. They've given us— Why, they've been incredibly generous to us! They wouldn't have done that—"

"Maybe," said Clark blandly, "they felt an obligation to act as technological missionaries to a backward race. They could meet that obligation and still feel bored."

"I don't think that's it," said Lucy again.

She looked very much better now that the Greks were gone. From the instant of the first broadcast call for Hackett and herself to come forward and be rewarded, she'd been uneasy. She couldn't explain the feeling, but it was there. Now the Greks had left and a vast relief filled her. It was as if she'd had an intuition of danger which now was ended.

The slow attempt at exodus from the scene of the ship's departure continued. The morning television news had reported 980 traffic deaths the day before, mostly attributable to the jamming of cars heading for the lift-off. It was feared that the toll would be higher today. Cars moving toward increasing congestion would be slowed as the congestion increased. But cars leaving a crowded area would make higher and higher speeds as they dispersed. The cars in the miles of parking space here, though, moved at the slowest of crawls. It would be hours before any significant clearing-up of this organized disorganization was achieved.

Hackett and the others went back to the tarpaper shed. The atomic bombs under the earth cradle wouldn't be lifted, with hundreds of thousands of people nearby. But the Army officer was greeted by a message from a high echelon of the military. While the Grek ship was aground, tests of the bombs' firing mechanisms had reported that they were dead; that they could not be exploded. But now, since the Greks were gone, the same mechanisms reported *go*. They could explode now!

Some unguessable principle or device had detected them underground, and some other unguessable device had inactivated them. The Greks had known about them. They'd ignored them—which could be indifference, but could also mean contempt. The point of the message to the Army officer, though, was that there was to be no effort to remove the bombs until the entire area was cleared of people, and volunteer bomb-disposal units could take care of the situation.

Clark frowned. "Ask if we can dig up the garbage pit now. It's nowhere near the bombs, and if we don't dig it out first we—hm—may not have the chance."

The Army man went away. Presently he came back. There was to be no digging within 200 feet of a bomb, but the bulldozers not otherwise being used could strip off the dirt cover of the garbage pit.

Clark was delighted. Two huge bulldozers roared and boomed as they came out of their shed. They went a long way around, and climbed over the excavated dirt that had supported the bottom tiers of seats. The big machine went wallowing into the great scooped-out cradle recently occupied by the ship from space.

Surveyors appeared. They marked off circles that must not be entered—four of them. The bulldozers grumbled and boomed and, under Clark's direction, began to dig out a trench a full bulldozer blade in width. It went down two feet on the first pass, more on the second. Like great, rumbling beasts of metal the bulldozers growled back and forth, and back and forth, while beyond the grandstands people were as fretfully anxious to get away from this now meaningless place as yesterday and this morning they'd been eager to get to it.

A hole appeared at one side of the trench. It was the garbage pit. The bulldozers attacked the side wall of the trench they'd dug. They nibbled delicately here—pushing away cubic yards of earth—and nibbled there to expose the pit.

As soon as the bulldozers were finished Clark and his three graduate student archaeological team moved into action. Carefully and even deftly they removed loosened earth, shovelful by shovelful. The garbage pit was a good twenty feet across. They couldn't guess yet how deep it was. At the top there were masses of wilted, still green vegetation, flung away as useless.

Clark conferred briskly with the Army officer. This green stuff was unfamiliar. It could be the prunings of tank-grown plants used in the air-purifying system of the ship. But it could also be terrestrial, if the Greks had been able to make air voyages of exploration without detection. In any case, it might not be dead. Conceivably it could be rooted and grown for study. Botanists were called for. The Army officer went to ask for them.

Then one of the graduate students turned up something. He had lifted shovelfuls of the wilted vegetation aside. He said in a choked voice, "L-look here!"

Hackett stiffened. Lucy looked, and put her hand to her mouth. There was silence. A shovel had uncovered a furry object, dumped in the refuse of the Grek ship. The furry object was the dead body of an Aldarian. Something unguessable had exploded a hole through his body. He'd been murdered and a shameful disposition made of his corpse.

Hackett felt a sense of shock. His throat went dry. He watched as Clark, very pale, took over the task his helper had begun. People liked Aldarians.

Clark found another furry corpse. And another. And another. They had all been killed with the same weapon. Then Lucy, choking, pointed. There were more bodies still. The supposed student-spacemen had been killed deliberately and partly buried in the ship's waste matter, flung there and remaining there in limp positions as if they'd been dumped out before *rigor mortis* could set in—provided they would develop it. They had been lately and violently murdered. Some unknown weapon had exploded or vaporized holes through their bodies. It became evident that they'd suffered other hurts before being killed.

Hackett said in an unnaturally calm voice, "This settles the question of how the Greks felt about the Aldarians. They despised them. They killed them and threw them out in the garbage. I doubt that they respect us very much more."

Lucy wrung her hands. She was now a doctor, and during her year as an interne she'd seen much that was unpleasant. But now she said brokenly, "Jim, that's the one we pulled out of the car wreck! See? We took him to the hospital and sent word to the Greks. And a Grek came in a helicopter and brought him here to the ship —and they killed him. Because he was hurt! Like we— might treat an animal that was hurt and—we couldn't cure. . . ."

Hackett said coldly, "No, Lucy. They hurt him some more after they got him back. And the others too. It looks like torture. And they tried very earnestly to get us to come forward and be rewarded for saving his life—they said!"

The sandy-haired Clark got out of the pit, looking very white. His three helpers seemed dazed. They'd spoken irreverently of the Greks, the night before, and they'd been zestful at the idea of learning secrets the Greks hadn't been inclined to tell. But however youthfully disrespectful they'd been, they'd revered the gray-skinned aliens. They'd envied them their intellect and their achievements—the idea of journeying from star to star was glamorous—and though they'd never have said so, they'd believed in the Greks' good-will. There was no other explanation for the benefits they'd conveyed to humanity. The three younger archaeologists, in fact, had idealized the visitors from space.

Now they looked as if they wanted to be ill. Hackett took a deep breath. He said urgently to Clark, "Go find Captain whats-his-name. Have him report this business and get this place guarded so nobody else can see what we've found. We're going to need more than archaeologists to go throught this stuff! The Greks have lied to us, and if they were only indifferent they wouldn't have bothered. If anything on Earth ever had to be kept top secret to prevent panic, this is it!"

The sandy-haired man nodded dumbly. He went in search of the Army officer who'd arranged for the use of the bulldozers before the atomic bombs were taken up. Hackett picked up a shovel and began to re-cover what had been exposed to the light. At a curt word from him, Clark's three assistants joined him in hiding from the sunlight what had been revealed.

Outside the grandstands the unparalleled traffic jam continued. One does not move a million and a half people—or any considerable part of them—in minutes, and the crowd present for the leaving of the Greks was even larger than had been anticipated. There was enough dust, now, stirred up by human feet, to make a fog through which it seemed impossible for any movement to take place.

There were collisions between cars fretfully trying to edge their way toward the exits and the complex of temporary highways that had been made for this single day's use. No one dared move faster than a crawl, so casualties were few. But the confusion seemed absolute. Dust-covered pedestrians tried to find the way through the glaring obscurity to their cars. Naturally there were car thieves as work, along with pickpockets and sneak thieves and psychopathic individuals seizing upon this scene of confusion for their private undesirable purposes.

People became separated from one another and considered nothing more important than finding each other again. Children became thirsty and could imagine nothing more important than having something to drink immediately. People lost their wallets and their identifications, and almost their identities, in such a horde of other people as no living man had ever experienced before.

There could be no priorities in such chaos. Police cars could only be used to make barriers by which what traffic did move was forced to move in planned directions. Military vehicles could only try patiently to go where they were ordered, when the crowds permitted it. In the special roofed, glass-enclosed section of grandstand reserved for prime ministers and heads of state and others of high rank, the collapse of minutely detailed plans for their departure had to be acknowledged. It was decided to send helicopters for them.

Then it was realized that the only place where copters could land was where the Grek ship had lain. But that could not be used. The bombs, of course.

The great statesmen of the world graciously accepted the situation, even though the bombs were not referred to. They chatted in the manner appropriate to high officials called on to endure annoyance. And hordes and hordes and hordes of crawling cars inched through miles of stirred-up dust. Some of them emerged with snail-like slowness onto the highways.

Many found it impossible to go where they wanted to, but went anywhere they could, so long as it was away from where they'd been.

But some necessary things did get done. Members of the honor guard protecting the foreign visitors were pulled away from that task and set to guard the re-closed garbage pit. In one place, close to the grand-stands, police cars were somehow formed into barriers enclosing an acre or two. The action created even greater confusion, and innumerable dented fenders, but helicopters began to descend into that small space. They multiplied the dust fog around it.

The helicopters brought very curious items of equipment. Canvas and poles to make a huge tent. Refrigerating units. The items needed to equip a biological laboratory for emergency research. Generators. Microscopes. Reagents. Even microtomes and centrifuges.

And there were three large copters which brought already cleared biologists and chemists and nuclear physicists and microscopists to the scene, and went away to bring back personnel tents, cots, food supplies, and such materials as would be needed by men doing highly varied research away from all normal conveniences. There were also FBI men to assist the military in security measures.

By late afternoon the ground was less than completely covered by dust clouds, outside the grandstands. At sundown, limousines previously held back began to carry official visitors away—often only to the nearest available airport. There was still a very great crowd to be moved, but it was possible to move motorcycle-

escorted limousines with reasonable celerity. But an
unofficial conference had begun in the glassed-in official area, and the prime ministers and/or heads of
state a surprising mixture of countries found it possible
to discuss certain items of international import under
circumstances making for flexibility.

The copter-brought equipment almost seemed to set
itself up for use. The lifting of the atomic bombs now
rated second in order of importance. A tent spread over
the pit. Other tents went up. Equipment joined together. There was power. Generators began to hum,
and lights were supplied.

Clark gave instructions on the practices of archaeologists making a dig, but he discovered that much of
his information did not apply. It didn't matter how deep
these artifacts and other discoveries might be, or how
they were placed in the pit. These were matters of
great importance in studying ancient cultures. Here
they mattered not at all.

Something close to assembly-line expertizing of material brought from the pit established itself. There
were nine murdered Aldarians at the top of the pit,
including the one Hackett and Lucy had tried to help.
They had all been tortured, and all killed, undoubtedly
at about the same time. The guess at the weapon which
made their wounds was that it was on the order of a
laser pistol. Only one Aldarian had the bone fractures
which would later make it certain that he was the victim of an accident who had been X-rayed in a human
hospital.

Lucy came away from the autopsy tent wringing her
hands. "It's probably our fault," she said shakily. "We
—made it certain the Greks would have him back. And
they tortured and killed him. Why? Was it that—thing
—he gave me? Did they suspect—Is it our fault?"

Hackett couldn't guess. He watched the swift and
systematic excavation. There were some rags. Some
crushed plastic containers which still held traces of
foodstuffs. Broken plates, of plastic. Metal oddments—
some quite reasonable, like broken knives and the like,
and some entirely cryptic. But there were no mechani-

cal items. There was much of the vegetation found at first. It looked as if there had been an excess of green stuff growing to keep the ship's air purified. Probably some part of the ship's food would be grown in the air-purifier tanks, too.

Ten feet down, in deposits of no special informativeness, they found another dead Aldarian. Lucy said evenly, "This is a female."

It was true. The Greks hadn't mentioned that there were Aldarians of both sexes on board the ship. This youthful female had not died naturally, either. She was probably about the same age as the crewmen that men had seen.

Two feet further down was a mass of broken-up crockery. There was also much foodstuff waste. Assorted trash. Three human skeletons, which had been alive when the Grek ship landed. They had been carefully dissected. The dissected-away material was found mixed with assorted culinary wastes. It gave some grisly information. The FBI was angered. The Greks had no right to kill and dissect human beings, however benevolent they might be in other ways. Then there was more vegetable waste, which looked familiar. A botanist immediately pronounced that some of it was terrestrial. They identified tundra grass from the artic regions. Dwarf willows, also of artic origin. Kidney ferns. These things did not grow in Ohio. The Greks had made explorations they'd failed to mention to their human hosts. Why?

There was an immature Aldarian, not more than half grown. His head was crushed as if by a violent blow. More trash, more cooking wastes, more broken objects—understandable and otherwise. Almost at the bottom of the garbage pit there were four more Aldarian dead, three male and one female. They'd died violently, too.

The ship had taken off at noon, Eastern Standard Time. At only a little after sundown the pit was emptied. Outside the earthen cradle there were still a great many fumbling or delayed individuals. A fair number had run out of gasoline in the traffic jam, idling their

motors for hours while creeping more slowly than a
snail toward the highways. But there were others. Important ones. In the brightly lighted glass-enclosed
part of the grandstand, informal but detailed negotia-
tions still went on between at least one ambassador
from behind the iron curtain and some prominent politician from behind a bamboo screen. They talked with
great care, but they talked. Doubtless they agreed on
something or other.

But there were still many thousands of ordinary citizens who hadn't left, and some who couldn't. There had
been crashes in the traffic jam. There were bent axles
and smashed radiators. Some had had to telegraph for
money to get home when what they had brought was
lost or stolen. And of course there are some people who
simply hang around where something important has
taken place. Not all of them are admirable.

Hackett went to get his car. It was a mile and a half
from the grandstand, and its contents would not be
particularly safe overnight. He and Lucy intended to
stay on here until something had been decided. The
discoveries in the garbage pit couldn't be made public,
of course, but something had to be done about them.
Since Hackett was responsible for them, he waited to
see what action would be taken. It wouldn't be revela-
tion of the discoveries to a waiting world, though! Most
people wouldn't believe them. They'd consider the
revelations as attempts to rob them of dreams about
to come true. They'd rage because such things were
said, not even considering whether or not they were
true. Yet something had to be done.

For one thing, Hackett needed to sort out his own
thoughts. He'd been ashamed of hating the Greks because they classed him as incapable of learning their
sciences. But they'd lied about that. They must have!
They'd lied about their crew. There'd been many more
than forty or fifty Aldarians on the ship. There'd been
members of both sexes, and children as well, and they
weren't aspiring students. The Greks had lied about
them.

They'd lied about being so grateful to Lucy and himself. The crewman on whose behalf they claimed to feel gratitude—they'd tortured and killed him, and then others. The Greks had gone to great pains to try to locate the man and woman who might know something about whatever it was that had made them murder members of what—it was blindingly clear now—the Greks considered an inferior race.

It was no less clear that the Greks considered men an inferior race, too. Their intentions could not be benign. They could not be philanthropic, as the world believed. It must be that they had some purpose they'd kept humanity from suspecting. It was probable to the point of certainty that they classed humans and Aldarians together. It was now unthinkable that they'd taken so much trouble to enlighten and civilize mankind, only to go away with nothing to show for their trouble.

So Hackett went to get his car while some conclusion was reached on these matters by persons in high positions. He meant to move his car to a better-lighted position where it would be safer. An FBI man went along with him. They crossed the now nearly open spaces that had been used for parking some hundreds of thousands of cars. The ground was inches deep in dust. If there'd been rain today, it would have been knee deep in mud.

"I still don't see how you figured it," said the FBI man. "Nobody else had the germ of an idea there was anything wrong with the Greks, except they were so generous."

"They classed me as a fool," said Hackett tiredly, "and they classed some fools above me. So I suspected that maybe they lied. If they lied about me, they might lie about other matters."

He paused.

"The trouble was to find a test to prove it. It occurred to me that they mightn't really be interested in us at all. And if so, it shouldn't occur to them that we might be interested in them, aside from what we could get out of them. But we *were* interested. We'd like to know all sorts of things. Even undignified things. And

I remembered what Clark had found out about the ancient Britons when he dug up their kitchen middens —which are really garbage heaps. So I thought it might be useful to examine their garbage. I suggested it to Clark. He liked the idea. So now we've all got cold chills running up and down our backs, instead of feeling pious and happy and confident that soon we won't have to do anything useful and can become permanent loafers."

Then he said abruptly, "There's my car."

A man knows his own car even in the darkness, especially if it's a few years old. Hackett's car was practically alone in a great emptiness in which rarely more than one stalled car was visible from any one spot. It was dark now. As Hackett moved toward his car, a figure came out of the dimness. There were no lights except those far away at the grandstand, and here and there headlights or battery lights where a car was being worked on.

The figure called, "Hey! Have you seen a Daimler roadster over that way? I can't find my car!"

The FBI man said, "No, we haven't seen it. It's hard to pick out a car with no lights, though."

"I can do it," said the man's voice. "What're you looking for?"

Hackett named his car's make and year. The nearly invisible man said instantly, "You're almost on top of it. Keep heading the way you are!" Then he said, gratified, "Ah, here's mine!"

He moved away and was lost in the darkness. The FBI man said, "That's queer!"

"What's queer?"

"He knew where your car was."

A car started up. As soon as its motor was running it rolled swiftly away. The FBI man said, "That's not a Daimler, but he drove it away. This is yours?"

Hackett nodded, and then stopped.

"I've got a crazy idea," he said. "It's as crazy as the idea that the Greks aren't nice people, after all the pleasant things they've done for us. Wait here, will you?"

The FBI man, puzzled, remained where he was. Hackett went to the car. It was his, of course. He opened the door, then reached in very carefully and switched on the lights. The instrument board cast some illumination into the front part of the car. Hackett came back. The FBI man heard him tearing cloth. He seemed also to be grinding his teeth.

The FBI man said, "Well?"

"My transmission—my gearshift," said Hackett, "is set in park. And I never use park. I leave my car fixed in low when I get out of it. Have you got a handkerchief?"

"Yes, but—"

Hackett showed him, in the vague reflected light of his car's headlights pointing elsewhere, that he was making a cord out of strips of torn handkerchief. The FBI man hesitated and then handed over his own.

"I think you're—"

"Showing signs of a delusion of persecution," said Hackett grimly. "Yes. But the Greks did want to talk to Lucy and me. I don't know what they'd have done if they'd found us, but I'm glad we stayed hidden out."

"But still—"

Hackett began to tear the second handkerchief into strips.

"In all history," he observed savagely, "there's never been a would-be conqueror who couldn't find men ready to be traitors in the country he meant to overrun. I'm talking wildly, but if you can think of anything wilder than we have to believe after what that garbage pit contained, name it!"

He went back toward the car. After an instant, the FBI man followed him.

He said urgently, "Maybe I can help. I know something about booby traps!"

Hackett said doggedly, "Somebody's shifted the gear lever to park, where it has to be if the engine's to start. Lucy and I would both be in the car with the engine running before I put the transmission into drive. So if anything is going to happen, it'll be when the gear is changed from park to drive."

He reached in and delicately put a loop around the small, fingerlike gearshift lever. He backed away, letting out the cord. He wasn't satisfied. He took off his necktie and used it to lengthen the cord. The FBI man said, "Wait!" in a vexed tone, and added his own necktie. The cord made of two torn-up handkerchiefs and two neckties grew pleasantly long. Hackett pulled. It grew taut.

The gear lever moved. There was a snapping sound. The FBI man tried to throw Hackett to the ground and drop with him. They were both nearly flat in the dust when the car exploded. It made a crater in the dry earth.

Hackett and the FBI man were in that peculiar area of shelter sometimes found around the edge of a crater made by an explosion.

The FBI man had a not very serious cut on his leg from an unidentifiable scrap of flying metal. Hackett had a cut finger. He sucked at it and had the flow of blood practically stopped when squealing state police cars came to a halt around the place where his car had been.

6

THE FBI MAN pulled rank on them and got Hackett back to the buildings under the grandstand from which the work on the garbage pit was being directed. The police hadn't been told what was going on in the cradle from which the ship had lifted. The FBI didn't tell them now. Eventually, though, the FBI agent-in-charge said very confidentially that a crackpot had made a bomb intended to blow sky high some of the dignitaries attending the Greks' departure. The bomb had been seized, and Hackett was to have carried it to a proper bomb-disposal site, but it had detonated from the vibration of his car. It was desirable that nobody know how careless a would-be assassin had been in making a bomb for political use.

The police were partly mollified, But there was resentment later when they checked that story with the crater and the completely fragmented car, and realized that if Hackett and the FBI man had been in it when the bomb went off, they'd have been scattered all over the landscape.

In the garbage pit headquarters the discussion following the exit of the local police was grim. Someone from the State Department took charge. It was self-evident that no Grek or Aldarian could have placed the explosive in Hackett's car. On this day, of all days, a member of either race moving about outside his ship would instantly have been mobbed by his admirers.

Actually, it was the discoveries made in the garbage pit which had kept Lucy and Hackett from going away in their car like anybody else. They'd have been blown to atoms when they essayed to start. But the bomb was more than a narrow escape for Hackett. Humans had placed it, and someone had stayed nearby to make sure the bomb wasn't wasted on a mere car thief or someone of that sort.

"I don't think that matters," said Hackett. "They tried to kill us and failed. It doesn't much matter who they were. We should get that object given to Doctor Thale. We should get it examined and find out what it is, what it does; why the Aldarian didn't want it found on him; why it apparently made the Greks torture and kill a number of Aldarians. The connection isn't certain, but it's possible. I'd say likely."

The State Department man said heatedly that some humans were apparently ready to commit murders by arrangement with the Greks.

"If things are really tied together as they seem to be," Hackett pointed out. "The Greks didn't know they wanted to kill Doctor Thale and me until they got the Aldarian back to the ship. Then they found out something. But they didn't know the names of the people they wanted killed until the police gave them the names from the accident report. So—what humans did they talk to between that time and the lift-off?"

The agent-in-charge nodded. "Good idea. We'll check

it." He spoke to one of his subordinates, giving him instructions. "What kind of explosive was it?"

Hackett grew impatient. The man who'd been with him discussed the explosive. He hadn't recognized the smell. It was a new kind of explosive to him.

"The Greks may have supplied it," said the FBI agent-in-charge. "No handy amount of TNT would have pulverized the car the way I'm told it was."

Hackett became more impatient. The important thing was not who had tried to kill him on behalf of the Greks, but why the Greks wanted him killed. The small, watch-sized object. . . .

Clark intervened. He explained that the object should be X-rayed with the smallest X-ray source possible, so there would be sharp shadows of the internal works on the X-ray film. It should be X-rayed from every possible angle, so it could be reconstructed if anything happened to the object itself. Then it could be opened; not before. This was standard practice when a mysterious artifact showed up in a dig. It should be a valid precaution now.

The FBI approved. Then Hackett mentioned the terrestrial vegetation samples that had been found. Arctic tundra grass. Dwarf willows. Kidney ferns. All cold-climate plants. The Greks must have some sort of flying device which didn't reflect radar beams. They'd been exploring.

"And if they were especially interested in arctic areas," said Hackett, "that would account for lack of observations by Johnson detectors. There's practically nobody up under the north pole scanning the sky for objects warmer than the air."

The FBI man who had been sent to check what humans had talked to the Greks between such-and-such times came back. There'd been ambassadors and prime ministers. . . . But at a late hour the Greks asked to talk to one particular ambassador. The farewell party was on its last legs when they requested his presence. But they'd talked to him earlier. Why again? Hackett said drily that it was after the broadcasts had failed to turn up either himself or Lucy.

"You mean," demanded the State Department man, "that they expected you to come forward, and when you didn't they figured you'd found out something undesirable and that they'd have to kill you?"

"There weren't many people who didn't know us by name," Hackett pointed out, "and who didn't know that we were wanted by the Greks. So if we didn't appear, it would look to the Greks as if we knew too much. We didn't, but it would look that way."

The State Department man said savagely, "As if we didn't have enough troubles, without the Greks having human partners in whatever they plan!"

Somebody said, "But what do they plan?"

"We don't know," snapped the State Department man, "but we know we don't want them to carry out their plan!"

The ranking FBI man said, "The ambassador who talked last to the Greks is still here. At last reports he was still chatting with the Ghanian prime minister. I think we can work this out, if Mr. Hackett will take a certain amount of risk."

Hackett nodded. It seemed to him that nothing was being done. There was too much talk. As a physicist he naturally considered that the important thing was to make an immediate, concentrated, all-out attempt to learn as much as possible of what the Greks hadn't wanted humans to know. They'd dismissed him because he said that their teaching in advanced physics seemed nonsense. It probably was, because they didn't want humans to understand such things as broadcast-power receivers—already supplying a lot of power, and due to supply much more—or space-ship drives, or in fact anything at all of Grek manufacture. But Hackett wanted to work in his own field, and fast! A breakthrough there—

"Of course I'll do anything possible, but I can't see that it matters who tried to kill me! The important thing is to get to work on Lucy's gadget and every other one available, to make a pinhole in our ignorance so we can get ready to do something practical. We're wasting time."

Of all times since time began, this was not the one to waste in indignation over the treason of a fellow human —or so it seemed to Hackett. He made an irritated gesture. The FBI man said confidently, "I'll fix this!" He moved to one side. He called his subordinates into conference, one at a time. One by one they left. Hackett wanted to grind his teeth.

Lucy moved closer to him and said in a low tone, "Everybody's shocked, Jim. They're confused. With time to think things over, something sensible will be done."

"There aren't too many precedents for that," said Hackett.

It did not look promising. Hackett himself was dazed by the completeness of the evidence that the Greks had lied about themselves, the Aldarians, their purposes, their intentions and, in effect, everything they'd told the people of Earth. And all Earth was rejoicing deliriously because the Greks had made mankind rich and Earth would presently be a paradise for the indolent and unambitious, and everybody had inherited a million dollars. . . .

Presently the FBI man came to Hackett with a road map. "We're giving you a car. Found the same model you had. Took it away from the man it belongs to. Emergency. You and Miss Thale—Doctor Thale—will get in it. You'll take this route. If a car seems to be trailing you—and it will—remember that we'll be behind. Also ahead. You'll turn off here. . . ."

He gave more instructions. Specific ones. Hackett said skeptically, "How do you know they'll follow?"

The FBI man said mildly, "Haven't you ever heard of a double agent? It's being arranged now. Remember, you're in the middle of something that's had the lid down on it, tight. This will work! And if it doesn't, there's no harm done."

"But if it does, Lucy—"

"She'll be safe," insisted the FBI man. "She'll be safe! Until the last two or three minutes there'll be traffic all around you. If we had time we could take still more precautions, but this will work."

Lucy said quietly, "Don't be silly, Jim! And don't say you don't want me to go along. Nobody else would do. And if this does work out, we may get all sorts of information."

"From them?" Hackett said sardonically. "They'll have been lied to, too."

"But we've already learned more than we expected, or they suspect," said Lucy. "Come along, Jim."

Hackett and Lucy had to show themselves. They had to do this and that. It was a task of some complexity to make sure that someone who'd been consulted not less than twice by the Greks the evening before knew who they were and knew that they were about to leave the lift-off site. But presently they got into a car which would almost have deceived Hackett himself. It was the same make and year and color, and very nearly in the same state of needing a paint job, as his own. Lucy got in beside him, and he drove away. Nobody said goodbye. If anyone noticed that they were apparently departing, there was nothing to prove it.

Certainly there was nothing to show that they'd had any part in the uncovering of evidence of Grek bad faith toward the human race. It was improbable, as a matter of fact, that anybody except the specialists called in within the past few hours knew anything about that. If the Greks didn't think of their garbage pit as revealing information they wanted unknown, it wasn't likely that any human allies they'd found would think of it. The only weakness in the plan Hackett and Lucy were to carry out was that somebody —the man who'd said he owned a Daimler—had seen Hackett approach his car and might have seen the explosion. But Hackett, indisputably alive, driving what seemed to be the same car, and matter-of-factly leaving the lift-off site with Lucy beside him. . . . Under such circumstances the report of his death would seem to be in error, somehow, and measures would be taken to make it come true.

He drove across many dusty acres which had been parking fields the day before and today, and would someday become a cornfield again. There were lights

to guide departing cars toward the permanent highways of this part of the country. They went over a
quarter-mile of horribly bumpy dirt road. When they
came to a single-lane hard-surfaced highway they
headed west, as instructed.

They overtook other traffic. Someone in the car next
before Hackett winked a flashlight at him. That assured him of an escort ahead. A truck came up from
behind and was content not to pass him, but to trail.
A flashlight winked from the seat beside the driver.
That was assurance, too.

He drove. Presently, at a left-hand curve, he could
see another car, and yet others behind it to his rear.
The moon was rising now. The car next behind the
truck was a limousine. The flashlight winked three
times in the truck cab. That verified that the situation
was developing as expected.

They drove and drove and drove. Twenty miles west,
a panel truck came down a side road and eeled in ahead
of the larger, heavy truck. Two road intersections
farther on, the big truck turned left and trundled
away. A flashlight blinked from the panel truck. It
could not be seen, of course, from the limousine. A
car behind it turned off. Other cars appeared.

"It's being handled well," said Hackett grudgingly.
"The limousine must figure the bomb didn't fire, or
that it was put in the wrong car and the wrong man
was blown up. They can't figure we're escorted, because our escort's changing all the time. And since
everything seems to be going like clockwork, we'll
probably pull it off."

Presently Lucy said in a steady voice, "I think we
turn left here."

Two cars out of a half dozen before them turned left
where a filling station made the road as bright as day
for a little space. Hackett turned left. The panel truck
behind him turned left after him.

"The others have gone on ahead," said Hackett, again
grudgingly. "And it looks quite natural."

The limousine followed the panel truck in Hackett's
wake. A motorcycle and sidecar left the gaspump at

the filling station. Roaring, it passed the limousine, the panel truck, and Hackett. It went on ahead.

"If that wasn't the limousine we're supposed to bait," said Hackett, "the motorcycle wouldn't have passed us. So we've been informed that everything proceeds according to plan. We've a few miles more to go. Are you getting uneasy, Lucy?"

She shook her head, but he felt that she was tense.

"This is well handled," admitted Hackett again, a mile or so farther on. "We humans can get very much messed up before we decide what to do; but once we've figured out what must be done, sometimes we're pretty good at doing it."

The car went rolling along the up-and-down minor road. Lucy said in a level voice, "Not much traffic here, Jim."

"Still too much for things to be spoiled. It would be logical for them to pull up alongside and blast us as they went by. But that panel truck will block them if they show any signs of trying it. Or they might shoot out one of our tires and stop as if to help us, then do something entirely different. But they'd have to get ahead of the panel truck to do that." He added irrelevantly, "I wonder why they think they're killing us?"

Lucy said nothing.

Miles down this lesser highway the car immediately before them turned right. That was the signal that they were to turn off at the next side road. Hackett did so. The new road went between fields and through a patch of woodland that was plainly visible in the now full moonlight. Hackett pulled something out of his pocket.

"Did they give you a pistol too?" he asked.

She nodded, as if she could not quite trust herself to speak. The panel truck did not follow them in this turn. The car that had been ahead went away. But the limousine did make the last turn Hackett had made. Suddenly the world seemed empty and menacing. For the moment there were only two cars visible anywhere —Hackett's and the limousine which followed it two hundred yards behind. There was no light except that from the moon and stars. The fields to right and left showed low-growing crops—cabbage, probably—and ahead there was pinewood on either side of the narrow road, which was practically only a track.

The limousine began to close up the distance between the two cars.

"Everybody's left us," said Hackett sourly. "We look like a burnt offering just waiting for a match to be set to it. They've probably decided to take their measures inside the woods yonder. That is, to kill us there."

He drove on. Lucy turned once to look behind.

"Don't do that!" commanded Hackett. "I can tell how far back they are by their headlights shining in."

The car went into the woodland. Straight pine trunks rose on either hand, with a minimum of brushwood at the roadside.

There was a crumpled newspaper in the center of the road. Hackett braked. He came to a stop exactly over the newspaper.

The limousine stopped just five yards back. Doors opened with a rush and men seemed to pour out of it. Then there was sudden, intolerable brightness. A pitiless glare made all the pine boles seem to glitter. There was a very harsh, rasping roar which was most inappropriate to the scene. The echoes of a pine forest give a remarkable quality to the sound of a tommy-gun aimed skyward.

A voice said, "Stop it! Stand still! And you don't need those guns. Drop them, fast!"

There were men moving out from among the pine trees. It was a really perfect ambush. The men from the limousine were completely at the mercy of those who'd waited for them here. Blinded by light, with the rasp of an automatic weapon to inform them what they faced in the way of armament, anything short of complete surrender would be suicide. They did not commit suicide. They dropped their weapons.

The ambassador from an iron curtain country gasped. He protested vehemently that if he were robbed—

"We're not robbing you," said an icy voice. "We're not arresting you, either. But the Greks wanted you to arrange a couple of murders. Remember? We're taking you somewhere to show you something. If you complain too much, as private citizens we can always turn into a lynch mob."

There was no confusion after that. None whatever—unless it was the confusion felt by the owner of a farm-house who saw the brightest possible glare among the trees of his wood lot and came to find out what had happened. He was bewildered when he was taken aside and soothed, and kept from telephoning the local sheriff until no less than six cars came out of his wood lot—one of them a very expensive limousine—and seemed to be welcomed at the main highway by an odd assemblage of private cars, a truck, a motorcycle, and a panel truck. All the ill-assorted vehicles moved off together, with the limousine in the center. The farmer thought, too, that he saw various peculiarly inactive figures passed into the various motor vehicles. But he didn't know what had happened. He never found out.

In fact, there was never any public knowledge of the fact that an ambassador of a foreign country, sacro-sanct by international agreement, had been carried bodily back to the place from which a space ship had risen less than twelve hours earlier. Nobody ever heard, officially, what he was shown there. But there is no question that he decided the Greks·had been less than candid with his government—even in the act of making a highly special arrangement for the very special benefit of that nation.

Hackett noticed that the ambassador was very pale when he'd seen what was to be seen. He was nearly as gray-faced as a Grek. He had members of his entourage brought there and shown what was to be seen. And they became skeptical—and afraid—of the actual purposes that moved the visitors from space.

Not reasonably, but very naturally, the ambassador was particularly convinced by a discovery just made, while his limousine was following Hackett and Lucy.

Someone at an autopsy table beside the pit noticed two small scars behind the ear of an Aldarian corpse. They wouldn't be visible ordinarily, because of the

furry covering of the skin, but these just happened
to catch his eye. The scars matched exactly. So they
were examined. It developed that something like a
scalpel had made a small, deep, long-healed incision at
those two places and had severed thick nerve bundles
leading to the Aldarian's ears. And every other
Aldarian whose body could be examined had had the
same surgical operation.

They'd been deliberately and artificially made deaf.
Obviously, by the Greks. These particular Aldarians
had been killed and their carcasses thrown out with
the ship's waste matter. Obviously, by the Greks. So
the standing of Aldarians in Grek eyes was specific.
To the Greks they were domestic animals, subject to
any enormity their owners might choose to inflict.

By some miracle of intelligence, somebody happened
to use the word "serfs" in the ambassador's hearing,
referring to the status of the Aldarians. And that word
had a very strong impact on the ambassador. It evoked
traditions and a bitter hate. It may be that the one word
had much influence on the future policy of a great
nation which believed it had made a private deal with
the Greks.

But this discovery, and all the information gotten
from the garbage pit, was kept from the general public.
There was little enough hope for humanity anyhow,
considering what the Greks could do, and our strictly
primitive means of defense. But there would be no
hope at all if everyone in the world went crazy with
panic, or if the public revolted bloodily against losing
its illusions. Some few officials in a few countries were
let in 'on the facts. Certain scientific men were informed. But those whom the Greks rated highest in
understanding Grek science. . . .

Those illustrious nitwits joined the rest of us in
gloating over the happy prospects we believed in. True,
these was much unemployment at the moment, but that
would soon be ended. True, even people who were
employed tended to stay home and loaf instead of
working, because soon they'd hardly have to work at
all. But—why shouldn't they loaf? In the United States

there were enormous stores of surplus food. The Greks had showed us a sinter field which made the mineral fertilizing elements in topsoil beautifully available to growing things. We wouldn't really have to work at farming, hereafter. Make a hole and drop in a seed, and that would be that. And we'd have free power and practically free food, and retirement at forty, with everybody owning everything he'd ever envied anybody else.

To a later generation our reactions may be hard to understand. But we weren't inherently stupid. The intention to murder Lucy and Hackett, for example, had been handled beautifully. We were quite capable of acting rationally. But not many of us did.

Even now we can act like idiots. Everybody. Of all generations now alive. It's quite possible that we may do so.

But if we do, we'll deserve what happens.

7

IT SEEMS to be true that all the intelligent races in the galaxy think more or less in the same manner. That is, everyone will act stupidly if allowed, and hell hath no fury like a population expecting impossibilities, when they aren't produced. The public expected paradise to turn up immediately, when it would have been impossible for months—if it were possible at all. So there was trouble.

The unemployment rate went up to thirty per cent. The number of people on relief more than doubled. There were crowds demonstrating and rioting in the streets. They did not demand employment, because that would soon be unimportant. They rioted for more speed in producing the perfect state of things for which the Greks had prepared the way.

Here there is still some dispute. Some students of the matter consider that the Greks read human psychology with a fine precision, and used their knowledge of us to plan their actions. Other students say that any intelligent race would have been as foolish as we were, under the circumstances. The odds are that the latter view is correct.

Some factories were shut down in order to be retooled for service in a Grek-oriented future society. Then they found it difficult to get men to work on the retooling. Most people decided to draw unemployment pay and wait until the factories were ready to hire them at a week's wages for a day's work, and frienge benefits besides. So most factories did not get retooled.

Some occupations and industries appeared certain to be wiped out. Filling stations were obviously on the way to extinction, with cars due to run on broadcast power. These cars were already present in considerable numbers. The entire oil industry faltered. The coal industry stopped. The building industry suspended operations, because new materials were going to make future building infinitely easier and cheaper. People waited for the new materials. Textiles we'd known how to make didn't compare with the new textiles the Greks had shown us how to produce, so the textile industry collapsed. And absenteeism went up unbelievably. There came a time when sixty per cent of the population was either without work, or else was staying home to wait for the working conditions that ought to be on the way.

Food was still needed, to be sure. But the return for producing and distributing it was not satisfying. Workers in the food industries felt that they should work only one day a week, as other workers were waiting to do, and they should be at least as prosperous now as the rest of the world expected to be later. Food processing and distribution began to suffer from an excessive loss of manpower.

Then people, happily engaged in waiting, demanded home relief to prevent starvation in the meantime. They were so many in number that they got it. The gigantic government-surplus food warehouses began to ship out food in bulk to nonpaying customers. Unemployment insurance funds began to dwindle. There was indignation that the benefits the Greks had brought us were not making their appearance in the life of the average man. There was suspicion of dirty work at the crossroads.

Really determined rioting began when a government ruling denied food to families of whom no member would accept employment of any sort. An infinite number of formerly tractable citizens found this outrageous. They demanded indignantly that what the Greks had made possible, the government should make fact, and ignored suggestions that somebody had to do a considerable amount of work to bring that about.

The business of government became simply that of trying to satisfy popular demands for the impossible. The government of the United States had been established two centuries earlier to protect its citizens against the unreasonable demands of a former government. Now it was forced to pretend to be struggling to meet the preposterous demands of its own citizens. Its really basic function of guarding its people against those disasters a government can prevent—that function had to be performed in secret. It had, in effect, to go underground to do what it was made for.

Obviously, with the world in such a state, the discoveries in the garbage pit could not be told, because mankind was drunk; drunk on dreams it would defend by revolt, if necessary. And if by any feat of reason the truth were driven into the public consciousness, the result would have been a mass panic a hundred times worse than the one produced by the arrival of the Grek ship in the first place.

But Hackett got an opportunity to work on the problem of the gadget from the injured Aldarian. It wasn't the kind of opportunity he might have imagined. Twelve hours after the ship's lift-off he saw an ambassador depart from the place of its departure. The ambassador was a very much shaken man. He had to convince his superiors that in attempting to sell out the rest of the world, it had sold itself out too. If he put the fact across, there would be a subtle change of policy. It would be a return to apprehensive cooperation, which was highly desirable. But his country might only pretend to change. And if it didn't—or even if it did—it might still think it politic to get two people murdered, just in case the Greks came back.

"There's no way to know," the FBI man in charge told Hackett, "whether you're as safe as you were in your mother's arms, or whether you've got a hell of a problem. But you'd better not go home. We can lock you up if you like, and keep you pretty safe that way. How about it?"

"I don't think I'd like it," admitted Hackett. "And there's Doctor Thale to consider. If I'm in danger, so is she."

"I don't think Rogers University would be a good place, either," the FBI man observed. "We could have somebody look out for your safety there, but—"

"I was fired from there," said Hackett drily, "for being incapable of understanding theoretic physics as the Greks teach it to human students. There'd have to be much explanation to the faculty, and I don't think I'd care for it."

"If you can take it," suggested the FBI man, "the best place would be one nobody could guess. Somewhere you've never been and nobody would think of, and where a stranger looking for you would stick out like a sore thumb. That'd be the last kind of place we'd send anybody, ordinarily, but usually the kind of man we'd want to hide would rather be in jail."

Hackett shrugged. "Suppose I ask Doctor Thale? After all, if the Greks want me killed, they want her killed too. And if the ambassador's government wants to please them, it'll try for both of us."

He went to consult Lucy. When he brought her back to the FBI man, she looked uncertain, but not depressed.

"She knows a place," said Hackett. "A tiny town, no more than a village. She visited there once when she was a child. Not since then. She has a woman cousin living there."

Lucy said, "She's older than I am. Her one claim to distinction is that she went to school one year with the

President of the United States. She always says it that way."

"Give me the name and the place, and I'll check it," said the FBI man briskly. "I'll only take a minute."

It was longer than a minute. It was nearly an hour. But he came back looking pleased.

"We've got a man who was born there," he said in deep satisfaction. "He knows your cousin. Old maid, eh?" When Lucy nodded, he said, "Everything's set. No loyalty check needed. The President's going to call her on the phone. Somebody'll come there to keep his eyes open for you. He'll get in touch with you. He'll arrange about money, get things you want from somewhere else, and so on. We'll fix it so you can get through fast with a phone message if you think of something."

Hackett said with some dryness, "I'm supposed to think? About what?"

The FBI man said cordially, "How do I know? Would anybody have told you to think about garbage pits? We've got a ve-e-ery tough job on our hands. How long do you think it'll be before they come back? Not ten years, like they said!"

"No-o-o," said Hackett. "Not nearly. In that time we could get over their first appearance. We might have developed some sense."

The FBI man shook his head. "That's bad! We've got to get a lot of people thinking. Like you. We've got to have research teams working. They're good, aren't they? Research teams? You hear a lot about 'em."

"They're good for developing something commonplace," said Hackett. "Not for concocting new stuff. They're really research committees. And somebody once said that a camel is a horse designed by a committee."

The FBI man grinned. "I like that! I'll get you a car and somebody to drive you. Had to give the car you just used back to its owner, with its gas tank refilled. You ought to get to this place where you're going about nine o'clock in the morning." He paused. "I'd like to say something."

"What?" asked Hackett.

"No flag-waving," said the FBI man. "Just this—we're pretty good in our line, but this isn't it. We're going to do everything we can, but the really important stuff is going to be done by somebody else. Maybe you. It's important, I'd say."

"So would I," agreed Hackett drily.

"If you and the others like you do your stuff as well as we do ours, maybe we'll come out on top. There's a chance."

Hackett didn't see that chance. In the back of the car, soon afterwards, driving furiously through the night, matters looked no brighter than they had hours earlier. We humans had incredibly little real information about the Greks, when one thought of it. They said they lived on one of innumerable inhabited planets in the Nurmi star cluster. That there were many different races on different planets there. That the Aldarians were among those races. That there was a well-developed interstellar commercial system, carried on by ships like their own, some larger and some smaller. There was no interstellar empire or equivalent organization. The Greks were teaching a class of Aldarian aspirants the arts of astrogation and interstellar commerce. There were forty or so such student-spacemen on the ship. There were a dozen Greks, as officers and instructors.

That was all they had told us. Most of it was plain lies. There were more than a dozen Greks, and many more than forty or fifty Aldarians. There were female Aldarians, and children. They were treated as animals, or perhaps as slaves. There was a time when human slaves were mutilated for their masters' convenience, and when dead slaves were dumped like dead animals, anywhere no one would object. Slave owners were not, on the whole, notorious for fine sensibilities or altruism. It wasn't likely the Greks had spent six terrestrial months instructing humans—and much of their instruction was deliberate nonsense—only to go away and reflect pleasurably upon the benefits they'd given to the human race.

And they knew more than men did. They had space ships larger than men could imagine building. They traveled faster than the speed of light. If they said they'd be back in ten years, it was probable that they'd be back sooner. They wouldn't wait for humans to reorganize themselves enough to use the new knowledge they had. The Greks would plan to come back when the old systems of production and distribution had been abandoned, and before practical new systems had been devised. They'd come back when they were most needed—

Hackett stiffened. One part of his brain surveyed the meaning of what had just passed through it. Another part said savagely, "Think of something, eh? Well, that makes it better than a guess that they haven't gone far!"

He found himself raging because of an opinion he'd reached without conscious logic. But he believed it. The Greks had gone away, not to let the human race benefit from their instructions, but to let mankind shatter its own civilization to bits because they'd shown it a possible more desirable one. They'd carefully and deftly made the wreckage of the existing culture certain, and they'd left without making the development of a new culture possible.

Given time—and not too much time, at that—the people who starved because they'd abandoned what they'd had for what the Greks only promised would need the Greks to organize and control them. They'd demand hysterically that the Greks return and give them the benefits that only Greks could give, and that now they couldn't live without.

There'd be no need for the Greks to conquer Earth. They'd only to wait, and men would conquer themselves and enslave themselves to the Greks, because otherwise they'd die.

Hackett may have been the first man to realize all this. The Greks weren't yet eighteen hours gone. It may be that no other man was before him in feeling the numbing despair the facts produced. When other men saw it—

Most men would never see it. Nothing could make them. Even if you proved it, they wouldn't believe it. Show it and they'd refuse to look.

For a few moments Hackett understood how a man could entertain the idea of suicide. Black despair filled him. It amounted to utter loss of belief in the essential goodness of existence. Because this was wrong! This was evil! It was not bearable!

Beside him, Lucy stirred. The car in which they rode ran swiftly down the road. Its headlights glared ahead. Fences, woodland, the edges of open fields flowed toward them and flashed past them to right and left. The car purred. The wind of its own making made thuttering noises, where a window was partly open.

Lucy said tentatively, "Jim?"

His throat did not want to make sounds. He said thickly, "What?"

"I've got an idea," said Lucy. "There are some Aldarians left behind. You know, the volunteers who are supposed to help us apply all the teachings of the Greks and make this world a sort of paradise."

Hackett made a mumbling noise.

"They know Grek science," said Lucy carefully. "The real Grek science, that actually works. They're the technicians. The Greks don't make things. The Aldarians do. The Greks are rulers. You might say they're the politicians who know how to rule other nations, like the Aldarians, and make them slaves. Earth may not be the first planet they've used this system on. What I'm driving at is that the Greks may know all about ruling, like the Romans used to. But they may not know much of anything else. The Romans used Greek slaves as schoolmasters and painters and sculptors. They had other slaves for manufacturing and agriculture and commerce. They specialized in ruling! But they overspecialized, which is a weakness. Maybe—just possibly—the Greks have the same weakness."

Hackett found himself listening with fierce attention. "Go on!"

"That's all," said Lucy unhappily. "I can't go on from

there. But it seems as if it might—have a bearing on things. For instance, the Aldarian in the hospital. He had a secret from the Greks. It—it could be that the other Aldarians knew it, and tried desperately to get that gadget away from him so it wouldn't be discovered. And they were caught and tortured to make them tell what they were about. . . . You see?"

Hackett said thickly, "Yes. That could be."

"There were women Aldarians in the pit, Jim. They'd been killed. There was a child. Murdered! And they deafened the Aldarians on purpose! There must be tension between the Greks and the Aldarians. I think I'm saying that maybe we aren't faced with one set of aliens who want to rule the Earth and all humanity. Maybe we're facing Greks who want to do that, and Aldarians who know what makes the Greks powerful, and, if they dared, would hate them. . . . That—might make a difference."

Hackett thought hard. For the second time in minutes one part of his brain thought of one thing and another regarded the meaning of that thing. The second knew a peculiar astonishment. Perhaps he was the first man to see Earth's situation clearly and to know the fullness of complete despair. But Lucy, who was a woman, had seen the situation still earlier and had gone past despair to find something that offered hope. It wasn't much hope. It wasn't a definite reason not to despair. But it did offer something that could be a starting point for resistance to fate and chance.

He drew a deep breath. "That," he said grimly, "is about the smallest grain of encouragement anybody has ever been able to think of, but at least it's something. It could be everything!" Then he said with a sort of mirthless amusement, "If this thing doesn't end with everybody dead, Lucy, I'm going to ask you to marry me. Not for your money, but for your brains."

Lucy did not smile. She settled back in the seat. "See what you can do with it," she said. "I'm glad you don't think it's foolish."

The car went on and on through the night.

At daybreak they passed through a small town.

Later, they found a roadside diner and stopped for something to eat. It was notable that throughout the tumult and upset of human affairs because of the Greks, it was the larger enterprises which became completely disorganized. Owners of small businesses—diners, service shops, country stores, little repair shops and the like—did not become unemployed. They had their businesses to protect. They continued to work even with the prospect of no need for labor in the near, though indefinite, future.

At eight in the morning they found a town of ten thousand people in which one or two stores were opening. At Hackett's suggestion, the FBI car stopped at a woman's shop, and Lucy bought things to wear, since her suitcase had been destroyed with Hackett's car. The FBI driver cashed her check instead of having the store do so. Hackett found a place to buy shirts and the like. Then they drove on.

Almost exactly at nine o'clock the car turned into the very small village of Traylor, which contained perhaps five hundred people. There was a state-maintained highway which ran down its principal street. Lucy looked absorbedly out a car window as they went along it.

"I remember that," she said when they passed a red-brick school. "And that's the town hall. Those stores are new, but that's the drugstore. I had sodas there when I was twelve. My cousin's house is around the corner. Turn right here."

The car stopped before a small and completely nondescript cottage with a yard full of shrubbery and flowers.

Her cousin was much older than Lucy. She greeted Lucy with dignity. "The President of the United States telephoned me last night," she observed with something of stateliness. "We had a very pleasant chat. I have a room ready for you, Lucy, but Mr. Hackett is a problem. So many people have come to visit relatives —things are dreadful in the cities, they say—that I couldn't find anybody with a spare room. So I've put up a cot for him in the woodshed. It wouldn't do for him to stay in the house, with both of us unmarried!"

"I'll try not to be a nuisance," said Hackett. "And it may not be for long."

"When the President of the United States asks an old friend a favor," said Lucy's cousin firmly, "it cannot be a nuisance. But oh, my dear Lucy! He asked me not to let anybody know there was anything unusual about your coming. I can't tell anybody he called me up. I can't even tell them he remembered the time when a naughty boy opened my school lunch as I stood up to recite, and I sat down on two slices of bread spread with strawberry jam!"

Miss Constance Thale, spinster, was one of the people who acted with sanity and integrity throughout the whole affair of the Greks. It is true that she was not employed by anyone, so she wasn't emotionally involved in the question of unemployment. She made no pretense of intellectuality, so she didn't feel it necessary to go out on a limb in ardent adulation of the Greks. She minded her own business. But when she received a request from the President of the United States, she wholeheartedly cooperated with the government of her country.

People like Lucy's cousin are very valuable. Those of us who made fools of ourselves remove our hats. We don't feel embarrassed about it, because they will never notice our tribute or know what it is for. They simply behaved as usual.

But we behaved like idiots!

8

THE NEWS reports, next day, carried long and involved accounts of the farewell to the Greks. They included post-recorded extracts from the tributes of eminent persons, and there was nothing to imply less than complete graciousness on the part of the Greks. Whether contemptuous or indifferent, the abandonment of the gifts just made them was not mentioned. There was some reference to the Greks' disappointment that two special human persons could not be found to receive the reward the Greks wanted to give them. But there was no mention of the bomb destruction of a car on the parking area. And there was no reference to the digging up of a garbage pit left behind by the Greks. There was total silence respecting all ambassadors— iron curtain or other—who might have tried to do a small favor to the now-departed Greks by murdering a couple of people they wanted disposed of.

Especially there was no mention of the garbage pit. It could be that no newsman knew about it. But it wouldn't have been published anyhow.

Publishable news dealt with the ship itself, which had been watched for by telescopes beyond the sunrise and sunset lines of Earth. It was seen clearly in Hawaii as a curiously shaped sliver of sun-surface brightness, moving out from Earth. At a hundred thousand miles it vanished. The Greks, so the news accounts said, were now traveling toward their homes at multiples of the speed of light. Their ship had vanished when that spectacular interstellar drive began to operate.

Most of the rest of the current events information dealt with riots and rumors of riots in one place or another. Congress and the Administration were under bitter attack for their delay in the extension of broadcast power, for callous demands that persons on relief actually attempt work for which they had not been specially trained, and for seemingly systematic delays in the application of new discoveries for the benefit of the average man.

The average man was a favored subject for speeches these days. Oratory had returned to the status of a century before. Merely suspenseful television dramas had lost their public. Something more exciting had turned up. Instead of watching while imaginary persons suffered imaginary sorrows for its edification, the watching and listening public had identified itself with an "average man" who had been supplied with a high and splendid destiny by the Greks, and was being cheated out of it. The regrettable thing about this picture was that people could believe it.

There was a further drawback, in that anybody who listened could take part in the worldwide drama in progress. And they did. Most confined their participation to words and grumblings, but many found it zestful to riot, to smash things, and, on occasion, to loot.

But these outbreaks of violence were restricted to cities, where people were much too sophisticated and enlightened to listen to anything that did not supply them with kicks.

In the village of Traylor, none of this applied. It was a small and tranquil community inhabited by people who liked it that way. There were no factories or industries. Everybody knew everybody else—had until recently. Nowadays Traylor was crowded with relatives who wanted their children out of the cities. Which was a sane reaction. It should be remembered that there were some sane people all through mankind's adventure with the Greks. Only they were not in the limelight.

Hackett found Traylor a highly suitable place for Lucy to stay in. Presently he discovered that her cousin had explained that Lucy had come to visit. Hackett was described as her fiancé, who had brought her here and had to wait until things settled down before he could hope to be employed again. She explained to Lucy that that story made everything look reasonable. If she couldn't confide to her friends that the President of the United States had called her up to chat and to ask a favor of her, she could confide something else. She had.

Lucy was unreasonably annoyed. Hackett hadn't mentioned marriage except when he said he might marry her for her brains. Lucy did not find the idea appealing. She wasn't pleased with her cousin. She was even less than cordial to Hackett when he came back from exploring the village.

"The Grek ship took off at noon yesterday," he observed, "and since then there've been two attempts to kill us, and we've been dumped here where everybody knows everybody else. That looks like quick action! But things move even faster than I thought. There's already an FBI man watching over us, and he's fully accepted in the village and not suspected of any special reason for being here."

Lucy did not answer. She was helping her cousin set the table for lunch.

"The answer," Hackett told her, "is that he was born here. He was pulled off some other assignment to come here and dry-nurse us. So he's officially on vacation and nobody thinks of him as doing FBI work here, because he *is* FBI!"

Lucy still did not answer. She went out to the kitchen and came back.

"I thought," said Hackett, "you might like to know that we're officially protected. But it may turn out that we're like a staked-out goat it's hoped a tiger will try to devour. If anybody can trail us to here, and does, it will be informative. But disturbing."

Lucy's cousin came in. They lunched, Lucy very quiet and Miss Constance Thale very dignified, as befitted a person doing a favor to her former schoolmate, the President of the United States. She asked Hackett about his profession. She'd no idea of what it might be.

"I'm a sort of theoretical mechanic," he told her. "But there's not much doing in my line just now. Nobody's interested in human devices any more. They figure Grek stuff will make them obsolete any day. And they're probably right."

"I do not approve of the Greks," said Miss Thale with dignity. "Whatever their intentions, they have caused a great deal of trouble. The President of the United States mentioned it to me."

"I'm afraid I'm causing you trouble, too," said Hackett. "But it won't be long. I'll be going away shortly."

Lucy stared at him. Her cousin said firmly, "You know what you are doing, Mr. Hackett. But I assure you that you are welcome for as long as the woodshed will serve you. When an old friend like the President of the United States speaks for someone—"

Lucy said uneasily, "When are you leaving, Jim? I didn't know—"

"When you seem to be safe," he told her. He smiled at her cousin and added, "When I've looked over the town and feel that there's nobody here who's likely to fascinate Lucy."

Miss Constance Thale looked benignly at Lucy. Lucy was disturbed. Miss Constance Thale read her own interpretation into Lucy's disturbance. She looked at once dignified and wise.

Lucy came to the woodshed later, where Hackett was pacing restlessly up and down.

"What's this about leaving?" she asked directly.

"It'll be presently," he told her. "At the moment I'm marking time. I'm acting under orders—the same ones you have. To keep quiet and stay alive."

"But you said—"

"That I'm leaving. I shall, as soon as I'm no longer asked to stay put. I'm developing an idea that I can't try out where I'm supposed to be respectable. I'll do it elsewhere. Then I can come back if the idea doesn't work—and I'm not caught trying it."

"But—what on earth—"

"I have an idea," said Hackett ruefully, "that might explain why we can't understand Grek devices. It's not a very sane idea. I doubt I can get anybody else to take it seriously."

"Can you tell me?"

He shrugged. Then he said, "How truthful are the Greks?"

"Why—I'd say not at all. Apparently not, anyhow."

"They said," observed Hackett, "that they were grateful to us for saving the life of that Aldarian. But they'd tortured and then killed him. Did they lie?"

Lucy nodded her head. It was not a pleasant thought.

"They said they were training the Aldarians like merchant-marine cadets. But they kill them more or less casually—women, too, and at least one child. Did they lie?"

Lucy nodded, wincing a little. Hackett said, "They've left now. They said they were going home. Did they lie?"

Lucy stared for a moment.

"It—it could be. I don't know. But it could be . . ."

"They said they left some Aldarians behind them as volunteers, to help us get civilized. Do you think that's the truth?"

"I don't know!" said Lucy. "I hadn't thought—"

"I like the Aldarians," said Hackett. "Everybody does. They do crazy things like trying to drive a human car in traffic. But there were female Aldarians on the ship—an item the Greks didn't mention—and two of them were murdered, plus a child. Remember? The Greks insist that they're benevolent and do-gooders. But maybe they keep the women and children as hostages for sons or husbands or fathers who are allowed to leave the ship. Some of them were allowed to stay behind when the ship left. Do you think they were left here out of the kindness of the Greks' hearts?"

Lucy stared. She bit her lip.

"N-no. I don't believe I do—not when you put it that way."

"You said you thought there might be friction between the Greks and the Aldarians. It was a sound bit of thinking. But if Aldarians are like us humans—and they act a lot like us!—and people they care for are held as hostages by Greks who will certainly kill them and maybe torture them if the Aldarians fail to carry out their orders—they'll fight tooth and nail for the Greks. They'll have to! So we can't count on much help from them. Right?"

Lucy looked distressed.

"That's terrible, Jim! But it may be right . . ."

"You know it's right. Do you see the point I'm making? The Grek are liars! And look at the fix they've put us in! We're barbarians! We use their sinter fields to increase the fertility of our land. We know why they do it, but not how. We de-salt ocean water with their apparatus. We know what happens, but not why. We use broadcast power, but we don't understand it, and humans use Grek-designed machines and make power receivers, but nobody can make out the reason they work. We're like savages staring at steam engines and tape recorders. We see them operate, but without a glimmer of comprehension. So I've got this crazy idea about why we don't understand. It's too crazy for anybody else to accept. I'll almost certainly have to try it on my own—and I'll get in trouble. And I don't want to be in jail if the Greks come back."

Lucy hesitated.

"Could you tell me what the idea is?"

He shrugged again.

"That the Greks are liars." She looked at him, uncomprehending. He said again, "The Greks are liars. That's it. That's all."

She frowned, puzzled and even a little offended because he seemed to have told her nothing. He grinned ruefully.

"Too crazy, eh? It's so absurd I don't believe it myself! Come along with me, Lucy. I'll buy you a soda at the drugstore where you had sodas when you were twelve years old."

"I won't!" said Lucy. "My cousin's been talking about us, and everybody would think—"

"They'll think pleasant and sentimental things," said Hackett. "They'll think it's a pity you've gotten interested in a man who can't even hold down a job. Come along."

She protested, but in the end she went. And they walked down a sunny village street, and he masterfully ordered her into the drugstore and to the soda fountain, and they sat on revolving stools and had a sticky strawberry soda apiece. And Lucy was astonished to find that the drugstore was smaller than she remembered and the stools not nearly as tall. Which, of course, was because she'd been smaller the last time she'd had a soda there.

On the way back to her cousin's cottage she said restlessly, "But what is the idea, Jim?"

"The Greks are liars," he repeated doggedly. "And if you really don't see it, it doesn't make sense. But I've got to try it. It's the only idea I've been able to get."

She hesitated.

"You'll—let me know before you leave?"

"Of course! And if I do leave, it'll be because I can't get any help otherwise. I'm not hopeful, Lucy. But everything has to be tried. Everything!" Then he said abruptly, "I don't like the Greks."

His expression was brooding. Anybody who knew what he did was apt to be unhappy. Lucy yearned over him, even in the bright hot sunshine, but that was neither the place nor the time to try to make his thoughts more personal.

The world wagged on. In Traylor there was sunset, and then a star-filled night which produced a slightly gibbous moon, and eventually there followed a morning and afternoon and another night. Hackett worked out his idea in detail and made contact with the FBI man who had been born and raised there.

There was an arrangement and presently he talked on a completely unmonitored line to the FBI man who'd been in charge at the time of the Grek ship's departure. He was told to call back, and he swore bitterly and almost did not. But he did, and talked earnestly, and was most gratefully surprised at the response to his argument.

He went back to the cottage, in great part relieved but again dubious about the argument he'd just offered.

He found Lucy.

"I could impress your cousin now," he told her. "I just talked to the President."

"What—?"

"I told my idea to the FBI character. It had almost occurred to somebody else. Almost. So they understood. They had me tell it to the President. And—it gets tried. You can help." He repeated, "They almost had it on their own. I'm not as smart as I thought. Anyhow they'll send me something to work on and put a crowd of really good men on it, too. No red tape. No taking the matter under consideration. No referral to qualified experts. I named it, I described it—and it's through!"

"But what is the idea, Jim?"

He grinned at her. "That the Greks are liars!"

He was elated. He grinned at her puzzlement, and Lucy was so pleased at his expression that she didn't press the matter. She'd know what the idea was when he had her help him with it. And he wasn't leaving. She didn't want him to.

In the then state of the world's affairs, people who knew how bad things were and how much worse they could become were not standing on ceremony. The decision on Hackett's suggestion, for example, was lightning-like. Usually when a high-level decision has to be made, somebody—or several people—will hold it up until they can claim part of the credit for it. But nobody wanted credit for obstructing the benign program of the Greks. The world was still celebrating the sure prospect of pie in the sky and the imminent appearance of the big rock candy mountains through those marvelous, benevolent, more-than-kind-and-generous space-travelers.

Which was why a highly technical operation had been carried out with incredible secrecy. The small flat object Lucy had received from the Aldarian had been X-rayed from every possible angle. If what it did could be discovered, many examples of it—of any alien device—would be wanted immediately. So the study had been made from the beginning with the idea of immediate manufacture.

After the X-rays, the object was opened with great caution, at a temperature far below zero and in a tank of inert gas. It was disassembled while motion pictures of the operation were taken. Every smallest part was touched lightly to the finest abrasive and the alloy determined by microanalysis of the almost unweighable samples. And while the device was being reassembled, fanatically exact duplicates of every part were being made. And then experts tried to find out what the original would do.

It did nothing. Nothing whatever. The small movable

stud moved. No result could be detected by any conceivable test.

Hackett's proposal was injected into the situation at that point. Parts for some hundreds of the devices were available when the non-operation of the original one became sure. One was assembled and sent to Hackett, while others were turned over to other cleared physicists for them to play with.

Hackett wasn't happy when the device was handed him. He wanted something made by the Greks, but he showed it to Lucy and she couldn't tell it from the one she'd received at the hospital.

"The report is that it doesn't do anything," he said wryly. "I doubt I can do anything with it. Maybe the Aldarians are honest. Maybe the original one got hit hard in that motorcar smash. A watch might stop from a jar, without showing damage that anybody but a watchmaker could see."

He sent a message pointing out that his proposal was for examination of a Grek device, not an Aldarian one. If Aldarians were truthful, he might find out nothing at all.

Still, he bought a small transistor radio and set to work in the woodshed of Miss Constance Thale's dwelling. He made a tiny screwdriver out of a pocketknife. He set to work to find out what happened inside the device. In theory, in order for any device to do anything, it has to use energy. In order for energy to be used, there has to be a difference of energy-level somewhere. He began to look for that difference.

He was perfectly well equipped. Any race might use screws. They were as inevitable an invention as the wheel. These were left-hand screws and very tiny, but his pocketknife-converted-to-a-screwdriver worked perfectly well. And for a check of energy-levels the transistor radio was perfect. The loudspeaker would make an audible click with the fraction of a milliampere of current. He checked it with saliva and two metals, and it clicked. He made two wire-points and began to hunt for clicks when any two parts of the tiny things were shorted.

It was simply a reversal of normal examination procedure. Instead of finding how parts affected each other, he searched for a difference in energy. Parts might affect each other in a totally novel fashion which might not be familiar induction or familiar magnetism or familiar anything else. Thoroughly capable men had undoubtedly searched for familiar items or principles in the gadget. Hackett didn't.

So he found clicks. When the movable stud was in one position there were none. In the other, they were there. He disassembled the device and put it together in every possible fashion. In one arrangement there were no clicks with the stud here and there were clicks with the stud there. That was all he found out.

Lucy stood by, watching. Presently Hackett said, "It seems to work, but not to do anything."

"It—might be," said Lucy hesitantly, "that it does something we never want to have done. A savage wouldn't understand a watch. The savage doesn't measure time and he couldn't see that the watch did. It wouldn't occur to him. He wouldn't understand a notebook. He doesn't write memos. So it wouldn't occur to him that the notebook held information. He couldn't detect it. Maybe we can't imagine the purpose this serves."

Hackett looked up at her.

"I'm afraid," he said painfully, "that you are smarter than I am. That's undoubtedly it. The Aldarians are smarter than we are, and they want something accomplished that we can't imagine. All we know about it is that the Greks don't want it accomplished. You're smarter than I am, Lucy!"

Lucy's expression flickered. A woman learns early that men prefer to be considered superior to women. And Lucy wanted Hackett to prefer her. She said nothing more—which was regrettable. Hackett stood up and gave her the small device.

"Here's a replica of a souvenir and it's all yours," he said wryly. "I'll report your opinion, which is also mine. But what I need is a Grek gadget, made by a liar, to see if I can get some truth out of it."

He was horribly restless as he waited again. It was unfortunate that Hackett had praised Lucy for her brains. It made her reluctant to say more than she had —and she had something more to say. But a broadcast-power receiver came for Hackett to examine. It was enormously complicated. He set to work on it.

This was the same day that an iron curtain satellite picked up fragmentary signals at certain parts of its orbit at certain times. They were not human signals. It could be he said, positively, that they came from the moon.

"Which," said Hackett grimly, "is quite unneeded proof that the Greks are liars! They said they were going home. They didn't. They're off on the other side of the moon, and they're keeping in touch with the Aldarians they left here! They can smash us. And they will when the time is right." Then he said very bitterly, "But they won't have to fight us. We can't fight. And it looks like nine people out of ten are already praying for them to hurry back and take over!"

We were. There's no use trying to pretend otherwise. We were impatient for what the Greks had promised and we were certain they could produce. We who went through the affair of the Greks find the current generation astonished by us. But they'd probably have done the same thing in our places.

They've had us to tell them how the situation should have been handled. We didn't handle it that way. There was no one to tell us. We had to play it by ear. And we did very badly.

9

IT TOOK two days for ground monitor units to pick up the beamed signals from the moon. They were on a frequency of which no human use was then being made. They were wideband. And obviously they would not be mere audible signals if they were intended for deafened Aldarians to pick up. So the monitor station

busily recorded them on television tape and then set
to work to decode them into presumed pictures. It was
necessary to figure out the number of images to the
frame, and then the number of lines per frame, the
scanning pattern and a few other things.

A few people heard about the picked up signals and
were uneasy. For some reason, security slipped up on
this item of fact, and a number of people noted that the
Greks had said they were going home, to ten light-
years away. But their signals came from the moon,
less than two light-seconds away. If, however, anybody
drew any particular conclusions from such facts, they
did nothing about them.

In the general public, though, there were no misgivings of any kind at any time. Not about the Greks!
They'd gone away after enriching humanity beyond
belief. True, there was unemployment, there was hard-
ship, there was depression and there was indignation.
Human industries, unable to sell anything but Grek-
designed units, and unable to make them, closed down.
Other factories, wanting to modify themselves to make
such units, were unable to get anybody to work at any
rational wage. People who saw the extinction of whole
classes of business—fuel, for example—tried to get out
of those businesses and the stock market hit bottom,
bored holes in it, and went down farther. But this was
not the fault of the Greks! They'd done great things
for us and they intended greater. So we were angry
and impatient with the current state of things. We
wanted what the Greks had given us and we wanted it
fast.

Already murmurings blamed the delay on Wall
Street, or capitalists, or graft, or corruption. People
said indignantly that "the interests" would keep us
from our Grek-given wealth and it wasn't likely we'd
ever get what the Greks had meant us to have unless
they came back and forced the arrival of an economic
millenium.

The point of which, naturally, was that people began
to link the granting of all our wishes to the return of
the Greks.

There was more rioting. In South Africa it took on a racial tinge. In ultra-socialist nations, the riots implied criticism of Marxism-Leninism. In other countries the rioters seemed pro-communist as well as pro-Grek. There was an increasing, seething political chaos in much of the world, and there was financial depression everywhere. Ugly moods characterized the followers of volunteer agitators, but also nearly everybody who'd set their hearts on working only one day a week with retirement at forty and everybody having everything that anybody else had.

The signals from the moon presently yielded pictures. They were of hands—Grek hands—making gestures in that formalized code with which the Greks communicated with the Aldarians. The pictures proved that the Greks hadn't gone away. But it didn't matter because the signals stopped. Hackett was among those who believed the Aldarians had heard the rumors about them, though they'd actually have to read them, and had reported the matter to the Greks. So the Greks stopped the signals.

At about this same time the various underground activities of the United States Government began to bear fruit. For one, Hackett found a way to find a way to discover how the broadcast-power receivers worked. He labored frantically at it. His basic discovery was that—as he'd guessed—the Greks were truly stupendous liars. Their policy could be summed up in a sequence of five statements. (1) If the Greks wanted to take over Earth, they could take it by violence or they could take it by deception. (2) But violence would reduce the value of Earth after they'd conquered it. Also (3) violence would leave the surviving humans filled with hatred which would make them less desirable as slaves. Therefore (4) it would be much more intelligent to let men conquer and enslave themselves so they would serve their new owners and masters with a loyal and grateful docility. And (5) the Greks' policy of action and of instrumentation would follow from the preceding statements.

They said they gave us all their devices and all their

learning. But their science was obfuscation and their devices were wholly deceptive. The Greks had designed—say—their broadcast-power receiver as a stage magician plans his card tricks and illusions, to keep his audience from knowing how he does them.

That was Hackett's basic discovery, after the way to make the discovery had been discovered. He examined a power receiver, not for its working principles, but for the equivalent of magic passes and mumblings that would look as if they did something, but didn't. Then he began to take such things away from the complex apparatus, and somehow to make their absence not count. On the second day he had his first success. After the third day he had a receiver that worked with nine-tenths of its original parts removed.

There were some other discoveries not reported in the public newscasts. There'd been suspicions that the Greks had some sort of flying device coated with a sort of radar black so radars wouldn't be able to detect it. In the garbage pit specimens of arctic vegetation had been found: tundra grass; dwarf willows; kidney ferns. The records of Johnson detectors, noting objects at a different temperature from their backgrounds, showed oddities that fitted in with periods of bad weather at the Ohio landing place of the ship. It became practically certain that the Greks had some sort of flying object and that they'd made explorations including arctic landings.

It was information. It fitted into other information but added nothing to the prospects for the defense of Earth against the Greks—particularly since public opinion was feverishly in favor of anything the Greks were for. Nobody would have taken the fact of secret exploration seriously. If the Greks wanted to go somewhere, why not? Shouldn't we let the benign, benevolent, beautifully generous and illimitably altruistic Greks do as they pleased?

Then Hackett ran into something which filled him with bitter doubt. Human devices, on the whole, work both ways. Radio receivers need to be changed very slightly to become transmitters, and the reverse is true of transmitters. Most pumps can be made to work as engines, and most engines as pumps. A dynamo can function as a motor, and a motor as a dynamo. The starting motor generator in human cars was a familiar example of the last. But a Grek broadcast-power receiver couldn't be made to work as a transmitter. It simply couldn't be done.

Hackett racked his brains. Until he worked that out he didn't have anything but an enormously simplified receiver. It wasn't enough. It wasn't anything. And time was working for the Greks.

No day passed without an intensification of the chaotic state of Earth. If it had happened without the Greks' visit beforehand, there would already have been starvation and worse. It was disaster comparable to war, when all a nation's productive capacity is taken away from normal use and applied to destruction. Now production simply stopped. It was not applied to anything. Prices fell because nobody wanted to buy anything, since presently they could get better things. Human production simply ceased.

Stored surplus foodstuffs began to run low. Many people began to hoard food. All other values dropped to zero. There was practically a complete paralysis of all human activities—and we waited blandly for the miracle we expected.

Hackett took his stripped-down power receiver to Washington and demonstrated it. It was enlightening, but it wasn't enough to start human activities up again. Attempts by other men to use Hackett's principles of research into Grek gadgets yielded no results. There were only so many human brains that could work on the premise that liars making machinery would make mechanical lies.

Lucy was along because she'd contributed to what fragments of information had been gathered, but Hackett alone made his demonstration and found out the inflexibility of most human brains. When he rejoined Lucy, his expression was queer.

"You look almost stunned," said Lucy. "Red tape?"

"No," said Hackett. "Everything's fine. I'm a hero.

You're a heroine. But—I've got a job to do. I'll join you later at Traylor."

Lucy stood still looking at him. He said impatiently, "I explained what you've done—how you've thought straight when nobody else seemed able to. You did what the Aldarians wanted. You kept your mouth shut and gave me the key to what I've figured out. If I'm—delayed coming back, somebody will come and talk to you from time to time about—things. What's been accomplished has to be kept secret for now, but you'll definitely be in on everything that's done."

"No," said Lucy. "I'm a girl—I'm not a Ph.D. in physics. I'm a brand-new M.D. instead. They won't ask me to help them. You didn't, Jim. I volunteered what I did volunteer. But I'm not interested in that!"

"What do you want, then?" asked Hackett crossly.

"I—" Lucy said very carefully, "I can work with you, Jim. I think I'm on the track of what that Aldarian gadget is supposed to do. I'd like to work on it with you."

"What've you found out?"

"Nothing," said Lucy. "But I think I've found a way to find out something."

Hackett frowned.

"I'll ask for some extra cooperation with you," he promised. "But you've got to go back to Traylor, where apparently you'll be safe. I've this job to do."

"What is it?"

He hesitated. Then he said, "They want me to look over a Grek power-broadcast transmitter and see if I can break it down to simplicity like I did the receiver."

Lucy said evenly, "There are two transmitters in the United States. They're broadcasting all the power that's picked up by all the receivers. They're run by Aldarians because we humans can't understand them yet. They're guarded like Fort Knox, but that's the story. Are the Aldarians going to be asked to let you putter with one of them?"

"No-o-o," admitted Hackett. "Since that satellite picked up those signals, it looks like the Greks are keeping in touch with Earth. So we daren't do anything that suggests we're using our brains."

"Then you can't see the generators?"

Hackett said uncomfortably, "Oh, I'll see them! That's being arranged . . ."

Lucy stared at him. "You're trying not to tell me, so it must be dangerous."

"I don't think so," protested Hackett. "No—not at all. There shouldn't be any danger to it."

"You're protesting too much," said Lucy.

Hackett spread out his hands. He said impatiently, "My dear Lucy, it's something that's done every day. People make a profession of it. I'll have expert advice. There's no reason to worry. I happen to have worked out a sort of trick way of looking at things—"

"Jim," said Lucy, "what is it you're going to do?"

He looked guilty. Then he grinned unconvincingly.

"If you must have it, I'm to sneak a look at a power broadcaster. Nothing to that!"

Lucy went pale.

"You mean burglary. Unofficially approved, of course. But the Greks have said the broadcasters are dangerous! They can leak a lightning-bolt at anybody who comes near them without knowing how to be safe. They've put elaborate alarm-systems around them—to prevent, they said, curious or meddling persons from being killed."

"But they're liars," protested Hackett. "So if they say they're dangerous, they aren't."

"Of course they're liars," said Lucy. "So when they say the alarm-system is to protect meddlers, it isn't. Jim, it's deadly! They don't want us to know things. They don't mind killing people. There were three human skeletons in their garbage pit! They tried to get us killed—and of all people in the world, you're the one they'd best like to see dead. I don't want you to do it!"

Hackett said insistently, "There's not a chance in a million that we can stall off the Greks unless we find out what they've got and get something better! The world's falling apart all around us." Then he said doggedly, "I ought to be back in Traylor in a few days, Lucy. See you then. Goodbye."

He moved quickly away. Lucy said, "Jim!" but he didn't turn. And she couldn't run after him. She was very quiet when the FBI man who'd driven them down from Traylor took her to the car to start back.

And Hackett went off to be instructed in the very latest techniques of breaking and entering, housebreaking, felonious entry, burglary, and the manners and customs of Aldarian power-broadcast technicians as far as they were known.

He studied hard. From time to time he took an hour off to attempt unavailingly to make promising young scientists grasp the trick of assuming that devices were not meant to be simple but deceptive; not efficient but incomprehensible; that they were intended to work only after bewildering anybody who tried to find out how they worked. A normal technically educated man instinctively assumed that things were meant to be simple and rational and efficient. It went against his nature to try to persuade him to the contrary.

"Dammit!" he protested hotly to four young men whose scholastic records were outstanding. "You have to become crackpots to try this trick! Listen. If a device looks like it works this way, it doesn't. You take it apart and find out where the design was tricked so that it looked important without being so. You assume that everything you see is all wrong and then find out what it includes that you can't see that is right and does work and is brand-new. That's the job!"

They were very conscientious young men. They tried hard. But as the time drew near for Hackett to try to look at a power-broadcasting unit, he was more and more disheartened. They could think with admirable precision about everything they'd studied, and they could use everything they'd been taught. But they had trouble trying to learn a new way of thinking.

Somehow, Hackett's depression grew deeper when he got a letter from Lucy, forwarded by hand through the FBI. It was a very friendly letter and he chafed at the fact. Its contents, though, showed that Lucy had every qualification he'd been trying to beat into the heads of others. The letter:

Dear Jim,

Something occurred to me. I've been trying things with the gadget like the Aldarian gave me. You agreed that it did something, but we couldn't imagine what, though it seemed it ought to be something we humans wouldn't want. I've been trying to think what they'd want that we don't. It occurred to me that they are deaf. Not naturally deaf, but deafened. The Greks want them that way. They can't eavesdrop and it wouldn't be easy for them to conspire, but they know about hearing. They used to hear. They might want to be able to hear again.

I found a patient of the local doctor who was deafened in one ear by an accident that severed his left auditory nerve. I tried the gadget on him. It is a hearing aid. Its cover is thin enough to vibrate from sound and it produces some sort of field effect that affects the ends of severed nerves only. If you aren't deaf it does nothing, and the same if your deafness is from any cause but a severed nerve. But it affects all severed nerves. I turned it on near a man who lost his hand in a tractor accident. He felt all sorts of sensations as if he had his hand back.

I think that if the Greks found out that such things existed they'd be merciless toward slaves who'd fooled them and who might be thinking of revolt.

I hope you're well and thriving,
Lucy.

Hackett wrote back:

I've passed on your letter. I would rather have you working with me than anybody else in the world, but if you think that by proving again that the two of us make up one smart character, it

won't work. Not this time! If I get away with what
I'm going to try, you'll see me immediately afterward. And I repeat what I once said about your
brains.

Then he angrily lectured everyone about him on the
kind of brains Lucy possessed, and the stark, raving
lunacy of authorities who put him to work trying to
learn from the lies of the Greks and didn't use her.

But he didn't want her with him now. He would have
wanted any man whose way of thinking meshed with
his own as hers did. But he didn't want her to share the
hair-raising experience he anticipated. The eastern
broadcast-power unit was in the center of a five-acre
enclosure. It was surrounded by an electrified fence,
booby-trapped and undoubtedly filled with capacity-
detectors and infra-red beams and such matters. It
ought to be simple suicide to try to approach the squat
power-broadcast structure.

Birds had been seen to fly low over the enclosure
and to vanish in what looked like electric-arc flame. In
some cases they'd exploded in mid-air, ten feet or more
aboveground. And Hackett had worked out a possible
defense against what he thought this might be, but it
hadn't been tested. It couldn't be and he refused to
estimate his chances.

But there had to be some breakthrough if there was
ever to be any hope of defense against a Grek ship a
quarter-mile long and with nobody-knew-what re-
sources of devastation and destruction in its hull.

There came the time when he was to make his practically hopeless attempt to find information that could
mean nothing when it was discovered. It was a night
with thick clouds. Far away below the horizon there
was a city which sent a faint yellowish-white glow into
the sky. An irresolute small wind blew in puffs and
lesser motions. There was the smell of growing things.

Hackett approached the electrified fence, trailing a
cable behind him. The fence itself was, naturally, electrified. It had been secretly tested earlier with an
electronic volt meter, which draws no current. No in-

strument within the squat concrete structure would report the measurement. Hackett now verified it again. The reading went back along the cable he trailed, to where sweating, uneasy men watched it affect dials and instruments. The equipment would either work or not. If it didn't work . . .

He climbed the fence. Nothing happened. He received no shock. He went down the other side. Nothing happened. The equipment he'd designed functioned as it should. The electrified fence had four thousand volts of ninety-cycle current in it. Hackett's body had been charged with four thousand volts of ninety-cycle current, exactly one hundred eighty degrees out of phase. When the fence was charged to so many volts, Hackett was similarly charged. When it was charged plus, so was he. When it was charged minus, he was similarly charged to the same potential. At all times he was charged identically with the fence. There was no potential difference between the two electrified objects, man and fence. He descended to the ground and moved toward the power-broadcast building.

The operation of his protective device made a sort of anticlimax. It was deep dark night. The air was warm, and soft night breezes blew irregularly. There were sounds of night insects, though not nearby. Far, far away a plane went grumbling across the sky. Frogs in some pond or other shouted senselessly without pause or rhythm. There was no sound which was not a natural one, no movement save Hackett's in all the world.

A faint light glowed. It was very, very faint, but it told him of high-voltage tension about him. He stood still and the distant apparatus and his special costume adjusted to it. He went on.

He heard tiny noises, more or less like leaves tapping upon each other, but not rustlings; snappings. Then Hackett saw tiny twinklings in the air. The wind had changed and now blew toward him. He heard a droning sound and a loud snap. Another. And another.

There were sparkings in the air around him. They

moved and surrounded him. And suddenly he realized what they were.

They were midges; gnats, mosquitos, tiny flying beetles and sometimes larger ones, and moths of infinitesimal wingspread. They were the night creatures which flutter and hum in the twenty or thirty feet of air just above the ground level. When an air current moves, they move with it, carried by breezes as the ocean's plankton drift where the sea's currents take them.

But about Hackett the tiny creatures were exploding in minute electrical snappings. A spark and a snap meant a gnat vanished. A hissing and crackling noise meant something large dying in mid-air and scorched to nothingness by an invisible electric field. The very air was deadly. But Hackett's carefully designed costume and the countervailing energies sent him along the cable were an answer to this intended form of murder. He wasn't insulated from the fields of force about him. Instead, he was supplied with counter-potential from the other end of his cable.

He approached the building. Three separate times the infinitely tiny light warned him to move slowly. Each time he was supplied with an electric charge equal to and identical with the outside potential.

He reached the squat building. There was an iron door. He opened it and found the scatter of an infra-red beam, slightly dissipated by dust particles in the air. He neutralized its power to give warning and went on, with infinite care and using techniques which were improvements on those of the most highly gifted criminals of the time.

Perhaps—perhaps—his crackman's work was less than perfect. But this installation had been in operation for months and there had never been an attempt to enter it. Every moment of every day and every night it had been under test by the midges and microscopic creatures of the air. The Aldarians had come to have complete, unthinking confidence in the protection against intrusion. There was no reason for them to look for intrusion now.

There was no movement inside the building. He

opened doors—doors are inevitable inventions, like wheels and screws and hammers—and they did not report his passage through them.

Then he came to a semispherical room all of sixty feet across and thirty high. There was a faint droning sound in it coming from a huge and apparently infinitely complex mass of metal, cables, cones and other shapes of dully glistening metal. Hackett pressed a button and tiny TV cameras began to send back fine-grain pictures of everything he saw. Hackett himself looked with more desperate attention and urgency than he'd ever looked at anything before. He saw this—that; he saw familiar irrationalities . . .

His lips formed furious curses. He saw, and it did no good. It was useless. He'd learned nothing.

And then he heard a noise. An Aldarian opened a door and came into the great open space which was almost filled with monstrous motionless machinery emitting a faint droning sound and nothing else.

Hackett froze to stillness. Aldarians were familiar sights. They'd been seen often enough on television. They were furry, with pointed ears, but they carried themselves erect and nobody had ever thought of them as apelike. This Aldarian crossed the floor as if to look at something in the mass of motionless, droning machinery. Hackett remained as still as the machinery itself. He was armed and could kill. But the return through the outside force-fields would have to be slow and cautious, and with many pauses while his protective apparatus adjusted to changing electric fields. Discovery would mean he couldn't possibly get back.

The Aldarian walked toward the huge machine. Then he checked. He almost stumbled upon nothing whatever. And Hackett knew that the Aldarian had seen him. He stood rigid for an instant, then went on and examined the huge device, turned and walked neither slowly nor hastily back to the door through which he'd entered. In turning, his eyes passed over Hackett and showed no faintest sign of having seen him. But they had. He went out of the door and closed it behind him.

Hackett waited, weapon in hand, raging because this adventure was meaningless and his death would mean no more. Because the Greks were liars.

But nothing happened. And nothing happened.

Nothing happened at all.

10

HACKETT TOLD it later to Lucy, back at the village of Traylor. He was somehow resentful.

"He saw me!" he said bitterly. "There's no doubt about it. But—he spared me, he pretended not to see me. Why?"

Lucy had listened very carefully, but she'd grown pale during his recital. Now she asked, "What do you think?"

"I don't think—I *can't!*" said Hackett more bitterly still. "He could have orders from the Greks. If they're contemptuous enough of us, they might think it amusing to let us beat out our brains against their cleverness, let us see their tricky apparatus. We'd never be smart enough to understand them. Not raising an alarm could be an expression of contempt."

Lucy shook her head.

"Maybe," she said in an odd tone, "maybe the Greks are more unpleasant than we think. Maybe the Aldarian didn't dare admit that he and the others had failed to stop you from getting into the place. Maybe the Greks would have punished them for that failure, even if they killed you when you were discovered."

Hackett growled to himself, "That could be . . ."

"And also," said Lucy, "it was a pretty remarkable thing for you to walk through screens and force-fields that even gnats can't get through. Maybe the Aldarians hope that some day the Greks will run into a race that's more intelligent than the Greks. Maybe that's the Aldarians' only hope, and you're the only indication they've ever had that it might be coming true. He wouldn't dare give you any sign of his hope. Maybe

Aldarians don't dare even trust each other, much less people like us, so all he dared do was let you escape so he can hope, though he doesn't really believe, that a race that is more intelligent than the Greks has been found." She hesitated and said, "You know, maybe it has."

"Not me," said Hackett savagely. "Do you know what I made out of what I saw of the power-broadcast equipment?"

"What?"

"That it's not power-broadcast equipment. It's only a receiver, tricked up differently from the small ones, but only a receiver. The Greks are such liars that when they set up power broadcasters they lie about it by putting up dummy ones! And we can't have the least idea where the real ones are!"

Lucy hesitated a long time. Then she said, "You said something once . . . You found there was power in the Aldarian hearing aid. Now you know how a receiver works, more or less. The Aldarians know a lot of Grek science. Could they have included a minature and very much simplified power receiver for the energy that instrument uses?"

"I'll see," said Hackett dourly. "Or try to! But what difference will it make if it's so and we find it out?"

It did not seem that anything would be of any use whatever. A day earlier, a delegation of assorted citizenry had waited on the Aldarians conducting the education of human students in the sciences of the Greks. The students had different reactions to their instruction. Some of them grew more and more unhappy as their human habits of thinking insisted that they studied nonsense. Others adopted a fine, idealistic attitude which said that it was not necessary to understand Grek science in order to believe in it, and that if one believed in it firmly enough, there would come a time when comprehension must develop. The Aldarian instructors did not teach this doctrine. Some of the students thought they detected a peculiar expression on their faces when it was mentioned in a burst

of fervor for all things Grek. But they permitted their
students to believe it if they chose.

It was to these instructors that a delegation had
gone. They spread out the world's situation as they
saw it. There was utter paralysis of the human econo-
my and utter loss of faith in human leadership, because it seemed to try to postpone the benefits of the
gifts of the Greks. There was such collapse of confidence that even paper currency had ceased to buy
things. The delegation begged the Aldarians to try
somehow to contact the Greks in their faster-than-
light travel to their home, to beg them to return and
direct us in the stabilization of our society; to beg them
at least to give us advice, to tell us humans what
to do . . .

The Aldarian instructors, blinking, read the elaborate confession of the bankruptcy of humanity from
mere contact with a more advanced and more intelligent race. The petition represented exactly the view
of the larger part of the human race. We who agreed
with it then do not feel comfortable now. But remember—we did not know of the garbage pit discoveries.
We didn't know the Greks were liars and the Aldarians slaves, or that Grek devices were one part opera-
tive and nine parts deception to keep us from understanding them.

The Aldarians asked questions, to bring out why
men begged the Aldarians to make us companions in
their slavery. The delegation explained. People were
on the verge of starvation because they had lost confidence in everything—even in money.

The Aldarians asked politely what money was. The
delegation answered, confusedly, that humans needed
a medium of exchange that everybody accepted. Paper
money no longer served the purpose. After many writ-
ten-in questions and answers, it developed that people
believed in gold.

The Aldarians seemed relieved and briskly proposed
to help. In the process of de-salting sea water for the
Sahara depression, to make a vast fresh water lake
where only desert had been, they had accumulated

vast stores of minerals. Every element on Earth was to be found dissolved in its seas. Naturally every one came out with the salt. The Aldarians brightly offered to supply any imaginable quantity of gold. They had de-salted more than a cubic mile of sea water and could offer some thousands of tons of gold. If more were needed, it could be obtained.

There was, of course, a complete collapse of all values that still remained. Even gold was no longer money if it could be had in any desired quantity. There was a total stop of business. When food couldn't be bought or bartered for there remained only one answer to hunger: Take it.

Some places—Traylor, for example—were far enough from cities to be free of hungry mobs. There were some organizations—Army posts, for example—which were held together by a combination of previous habit and discipline. But our human civilization began to go downhill and fast.

But again, just as the one-man businesses did not collapse with the larger ones, so there were still people who behaved sanely as individuals, as families, and sometimes even larger groups. All over the world there were tumults and lootings and unorganized disorder, but also all over the world there were humans who reacted to this disaster as they would have reacted to an earthquake or a plague, sanely and with courage. And this human fraction would be available if any hope sprang up. It was not, on the whole, very well represented in the first delegation to ask for the return of the Greks.

There was a curious side effect from the complexity of the Grek devices. On the East Coast a Grek fish-herding device ceased to work and there was panic in the population near one estuary, because a large part of the food supply there was fish. It was simple, stark necessity that the herder be gotten back to work. The proprietor of a television repair shop undertook the work. He took the fish-herding unit apart and put it together again. It worked. He'd puttered with it ignorantly and had a number of parts left over, but it worked.

A garage mechanic tried to reconstruct a sinter-field generator, knocked out of operation and partly crushed by a collision of the truck that carried it. He stripped it down, straightened out bent parts and found some parts that were ruined, destroyed. He began to reassemble it, checking the way current went through it as he put back each part. It began to work when by Grek standards it was only partly complete. The garage mechanic found it embarrassingly efficient. It not only loosened the chemical bonds of minerals, so plants could make use of fertilizing elements formerly locked up in topsoil but it reduced metals to powder. He had to put extra, unnecessary parts back to throttle down its activity.

Word got to the FBI and somebody had an inspiration. Every office of that organization was informed that it was at least as important to get information about repairs to Grek devices as to arrest low number public enemies. Trickles of information began to come in. Some of them were disheartening. One was that sinter fields, in making any amount of fertilizing elements available to crops, made the same amount of fertilizer available to weeds. Agriculture was not simplified to a mere making of holes and dropping seeds in them. Bigger and better weeds were consequences of Grek technology in agriculture.

Very curious results turned up as a consequence of enthusiastic but uninformed putterings with Grek machinery. A new laser principle turned up in a high school science laboratory and burned down half a high school before it could be gotten under control. Somebody else bewilderedly displayed something which could only be described as the fractional distillation of isotopes. Such things were admirable, but they didn't apply to the big problem on which the fate of humanity depended.

Even Hackett puttered fretfully in the woodshed of Lucy's Cousin Constance. He resented the unscientific methods he was using, but there was no scientific way to attack the problem. The human race had to have one thing if it was to have any hope of resisting the Greks. It had to have power that the Greks couldn't turn off. Human generating plants were abandoned and power distribution networks were gone down the drain for lack of maintainance. The Greks could cut off three-quarters of the world's power supply at will. We humans didn't even know where it was generated!

So Hackett puttered. He searched harassedly and almost at random for some portion of some Grek device that wouldn't look like itself—itself being a way to get power out of anything at all. We know now that his whole notion was wrong, but the odds were astronomically against us anyhow.

And naturally, at just this time a more than usually depressing development would have to appear. Hackett had been one of those to insist that the skies ought to be watched more carefully. Apparatus had been improvised. Wide-angle Schmidt telescopes were set to work forming temperature images of the sky. Johnson detectors scanned the images for spots whose temperature was above normal for the background.

They picked up a moving higher temperature area almost at the edge of the moon and actually just as it came out from behind it. It did not reflect sunlight. No telescope could pick it up, but it could be tracked. Something warmer than interplanetary space moved toward Earth from the moon. It was radar black.

Johnson detectors trailed it to a halt some thousands of miles out from the arctic regions. It hovered there as if making certain no new strange frequency played upon it.

It descended. No human eye saw it, but the detectors that amplified infra-red as if it were microwaves triangulated its descent. It stayed aground for some days, then rose once more and went around the bulge of the Earth, down the middle of the Pacific. There were jet planes racing it to the antarctic, but they lost. They had Johnson detectors, however, at work when it rose once more and went deliberately back to the moon. There were guesses that since signals from the moon had been picked up by men, physical communication was desirable for the time being.

Then Hackett discovered that a curiously formed small metal part in the Aldarian hearing aid looked very much like a larger part in a broadcast-power receiver. It was a fishlike shape, extraordinarily resembling one of the figures in the Tao, the Chinese symbol of the eternal way. In the power-receiver it performed a function, carrying current from one place to another. Its peculiar shape allowed it to do so without shorting anything. In the Aldarian device the piece of metal was smaller—much smaller—but was identical in shape except at the pointed end. There the two elements of the two devices differed markedly. That pointed end was the spot where the broadcast receiver appeared to deliver usable current. And the force-field of the Aldarian device, the energy-field, the whatever-it-was that affected severed nerves, appeared to come into existence at the corresponding differently shaped pointed end.

Lucy watched as he sweated over the cryptic, comparable parts. She acted oddly, these days. She seemed relieved when he straightened up, shaking his head helplessly.

"It takes power from nowhere," he said, "but we almost understand that. Then the same power—it must be the same power—comes out of the apparatus in the one case as something that affects only cut nerves, and in the other it's perfectly normal high-frequency current we can rectify and use!"

Lucy watched his face. She said tentatively, "Nerves are pretty much alike in some ways, as electric conductors are. Stimulate an optic nerve by any means and you see a flash of light. Give the same stimulus to a taste bud and you have taste. Pain nerves will report pain from the same stimulus that reported as light, taste, and so on. It's not the stimulus given to a nerve or a wire that determines what happens. It's what the nerve or wire leads to."

He looked up at her blankly. Then his eyes grew shrewd.

"Go on!"

"Go on with what?" asked Lucy.

"You've got the answer I haven't found," said Hackett. "I think you've had it for some time. I can't find it —tell me."

Lucy hesitated.

"Come on!" he insisted. "Come on! You try to keep me from realizing how many brains you have, but you aren't smart enough. You can't fool me on a thing like this. I can read you like a book."

"You can? I don't think so!"

"You were hinting at the answer then. You were trying to make me think of something that's all clear in your own mind." He grinned suddenly. "Do that, Lucy, and I'll prove I can read you like a book!"

She looked at him for a long time, studying his expression.

"It isn't all clear," she said defensively, and untruthfully. "But that piece of metal could be, for most of its length, like a nerve. Broadcast power—whatever that is!—goes into the thick rounded end of it. But the thin ends are shaped differently in the two instruments, and they don't need to be if they're only current carriers. I said that one nerve makes a sensation of light and another of pain and so on, depending on what it goes to."

"So?" said Hackett.

"I wonder," said Lucy reluctantly, "if you made a new small piece to fit in the hearing aid, and shaped it like the piece from the power receiver—I wonder if it would turn the hearing aid into a power receiver?"

Hackett's grin went awry. He shook his head and stood up.

"You mean," he told her, "that the shape in general transforms the broadcast power—whatever it is—but the shape of the thin end determines what it's transformed into." Then he said vexedly, "I'm the damnedest idiot, Lucy—"

He reached out his hands and drew her to him. He kissed her thoroughly. For an instant she resisted, then she didn't.

"I'm a damned idiot for not doing that before," he said a moment later.

"N-no," said Lucy, rather breathless. "But when you did that, you—did read me like a book!"

"We'll prove that you're right about the gadget," said Hackett, "after one more short paragraph."

Presently they were smiling at each other quite absurdly. Hackett said, "It seemed there wasn't any use in anything, Lucy. I didn't want to be sure about you because I thought this business of the Greks was hopeless. And if it was, I meant to get killed because—"

"We'll win now," said Lucy confidently.

"Now," he told her, "we've got to! Stay here and watch while I prove how beautifully your idea works. It's going to make all the difference in the world."

It took him all of half an hour to make a minute, curled up, fish-shaped sliver of metal perhaps three-quarters of an inch long. It was exactly like the one in the Aldarian device except for the last sixteenth of an inch. There its shape was that of the corresponding part of the power receiver.

He assembled it into the tiny, watch-shaped object. He moved the stud.

There was the smell of hot metal. The device that had formerly affected severed nerves no longer did anything of the sort. Instead, it took broadcast power from somewhere and turned out electric current enough to melt itself down if Hackett hadn't hastily turned it off.

A second delegation of citizens went to the Aldarians about now. Hackett didn't know of it at the time. He was in Washington, feverishly showing what he'd found out, demanding a sinter-field generator and listening to other feverish men trying to fit something they'd discovered into something somebody else had found out. They were shunted into the red brick Smithsonian lecture hall as a place for them to argue together.

Hackett pulled down a sinter-field generator. He had a substitute part corresponding to a part from a power receiver. He switched the substitute for the original part and the sinter-field generator became a power receiver. He switched another substitute into the Aldarian hearing aid and it became a sinter-field generator.

His demonstration was conclusive and started a tumultuous interchange of enthusiastic views and deductions.

"Doctor Thale," said Hackett pugnaciously, "is responsible for this particular development. She is convinced that the Greks are not our superiors in intelligence. She believes that at some time in the past they had a lucky break. A couple of hundred years ago we discovered the principle of the dynamo and the motor. Modern human civilization depends absolutely upon that principle. The Greks found something else. And their civilization depends on this! They found a way to put power into the air and they found a way to get it out again. And in getting it out, they found it could take innumerable forms. One was standard electric current. One herds fish. One is a sinter field." He stopped and said deliberately, "One may be—must be —unidirectional thrust. A space drive."

A unidirectional thrust would push a ship through emptiness. Babblings came from everywhere. Now research had a purpose and a program. It was to make as many metal instrument parts as possible with different shapes at their pointed ends, and see what they produced. Nobody could guess, but everybody wanted to find out.

Hackett was leaving the room, almost fighting his way through men who wanted to buttonhole him, when the FBI man of the lift-off site came to his rescue. He got Hackett outside.

"I've got a job for you," he said cordially. "Want to hear the details?"

"I've got plenty to do," Hackett told him. "What's the job?"

"Civilian adviser," said the FBI man blandly, "to an exercise of ski troops. We know where something from the moon landed and stayed a couple of days and then lifted off again. Since what we thought were power-broadcasting stations aren't—as you discovered—maybe the real ones are up in the arctic, where this thing landed for awhile."

Hackett said, "I'm getting a little bit fed up with being ordered around."

"Ordered?" said the FBI man. "This is no order—this is an opportunity! Don't you want to take a look at a real power-broadcasting unit?"

Hackett said hungrily, "I was planning to try—I'll have to—Naturally!"

He might have to argue with Lucy. She attempted sometimes, now, to act in a proprietary fashion. She wouldn't want him to go into danger, but everybody was in danger. If the Greks came back, very many people would zestfully submit to them in the expectation of working only one day a week and retiring at forty, and so on. When they didn't get into that blissful state, they'd want to revolt. Considering the nature of human beings, a very great many of them would need to be killed before the balance were as subjugated as the Aldarians. And they weren't too much subdued to dream of disaster to their masters.

So Hackett undertook to go with a fast-moving small expedition into the arctic on the same day a second delegation went to the Aldarians to plead for their intercession with the Greks. The people of Earth begged them to return, on any terms they chose. They'd left gifts on Earth, and the rulers of Earth withheld them and oppressed the poor, and there was no one that humanity could turn to but the Greks—the benign, the generous, the infinitely admirable and altruistic Greks! Let the Greks come back. Let them establish that paradisiacal state of things they meant humanity to enjoy. Unless they returned, their benefactions would be useless.

The Aldarians to whom this second petition was presented read it carefully. They replied in writing that they had not yet been able to reach the Greks on their homeward way. Communication with a ship traveling faster than light was a tricky business, but they would continue to try. When they made contact with the

Greks, they would tell humanity what the reply was. Hackett knew nothing of this. He was busy.

In three hours he was in a jet plane lifting off for Fairbanks, Alaska. There he'd take a plane—a slower plane—to a bush pilots' airstrip in Baffin Land. There were heavy-duty helicopters already heading to meet the expedition there. The expedition would be volunteers with some arctic training, and the copters would fly them as low as they dared toward the northwest and as near the shores of Morrow Island as a flying craft would dare. The thing from the moon had landed there. Its landing place could be spotted certainly within a ten-mile area, and probably within one. What would happen when the small party got there might well determine the fate of the human race. If it was successful, the chances were good. If it failed, we humans would be no worse off. We couldn't be much worse off! It was up to Hackett, to the twenty troopers with arctic training, and to two Eskimos and their dog teams carrying supplies.

Hackett landed at Fairbanks, took off again with some very competent young soldiers in troop carrier planes, flew north through dusky twilight and into night that became complete as the sun slid sidewise down below the horizon, and landed at a completely inadequate airstrip on Baffin Land. There were huge helicopters waiting for them.

They flew through blackness at the time the Aldarians politely reported that they had made good contact with the swiftly traveling Grek ship, incredible billions of miles away and going farther. The Greks would give the human plea for their return the most indulgent consideration. They would let humanity know what they'd decided shortly. Meanwhile they went on away from Earth.

A clamour arose, demanding that the Greks be persuaded to come back at any cost, under any considerations. While the Greks were here, marvelous things happened. Everybody inherited a million dollars, everybody was going to be rich. When they left everything went wrong, there was no work, there was no food.

Paraders displayed banners inscribed GREKS COME HOME! and requested the Aldarians to notify the Greks of this public and unanimous demand for their return.

We who did not protest this attitude, and especially those of us who took part in those futile demonstrations, are not pleased with ourselves now. But considering the information we had, it was reasonable. Considering how we'd have reacted if we'd known what Hackett and some hundreds of other secretive persons knew, it was reasonable for us to be kept in ignorance. The fact that men are rational animals doesn't mean they can't be stupid on occasion. We were. We tell about it to keep other generations from being stupid in the same fashion.

Unfortunately it's only too likely that they'll simply behave like idiots about something else.

Anyhow, while most of the world paraded and demonstrated and expressed the most passionate possible desire for the return of the Greks, Hackett and his entirely inadequate army moved through the arctic night. The Northern Lights flickered overhead, and sometimes they were overbright for people who did not want to be seen though the throbbing of the copters could be heard for many miles.

Eventually they landed and took up their journey on foot. Then when the copters were gone, they were in a world of frozen silence. Sometimes pack ice somewhere growled for no reason except to break the stillness. Sometimes when the lights were brightest it seemed that the faintest of hissing, whispering noises came down from where the aurora played. But they went on at the best speed possible.

At best their traveling was laborious past imagining, and there were unseen perils, as when one of their number vanished without sound or outcry, and they backtracked and found where he'd gone through snow that had held the rest of them, down into a crevasse on an unsuspected semi-glacier.

It was daunting to move through a night that never lifted, in cold so bitter that no word for it was known, in a world which was mostly noiseless, yet which sometimes made abrupt harsh sounds for which no reason could be assigned. They traveled doggedly, in the dark and over rough and broken ice. They rested in the bitter chill of night. They waked in darkness and went on in darkness.

It was a nightmare. Their mission itself had the feeling of total unreality. They knew nothing of events except where they struggled desperately to cover distance swiftly in a blackness that never lifted. There was a shortwave set on one of the dogsleds, but it would not be wise to use it, not even for reception of broadcast news. Resonant receivers can be detected. So they did not know when, after days of seeming hesitation, the Greks appeared to agree to return to Earth.

On the fifth day's—night's—journeying they saw a light far away. It glowed for perhaps two minutes, the only light or sign of life in any form that they'd seen in two hundred miles. Then it went out.

Hackett and his small party moved onward with redoubled caution. There was life here—the light proved it.

It would be an installation armed and guarded, designed to help in the subjugation of the Earth and the enslavement of its population, with that population's wildly enthusiastic approval.

11

COLD, ICY stars filled the firmament. They shone upon a faintly visible icescape which was totally un-unlike the planet Earth as Hackett had known it before. Even the sky was strange, because the Big Dipper was almost directly overhead and the Milky Way was strangely placed as well. There were no trees and no grass. The air entering one's nostrils was intolerably frigid. Hackett himself wore white outer garments over clumsy inner ones, white garments so he would be inconspicuous! The dogs were muzzled, muted lest they bark or snarl. The dog whips were lashed to the two sledges lest the Eskimo dog drivers forget the need for absolute silence. Sometimes, not often, a dog whined. But there were crunching sounds where men on snowshoes moved about on utterly brittle snow.

It occurred to Hackett that perhaps the precautions for silence were ridiculous, if only deaf Aldarians manned this hidden refuge. But there might not be only Aldarians; there'd been something which came from the moon. The Grek ship undoubtedly waited there. Greks could have journeyed to Earth in that space vehicle, whatever it happened to be. If Aldarians were their slaves, they would be sharply and suspiciously watched. There'd been reason, in Grek eyes, for the torture and murder and contemptuous burial in ship garbage of a number of them before the ship lifted off. The Greks would watch for other thoughts of insubordination. They'd look for failure of alertness and obedience. It was not impossible that one or more Greks would remain at this establishment.

And if one were, they'd be fighting with human powder-weapons against unguessable instruments of destruction in the hands of the Grek. They had weapons, certainly. The murdered Aldarians had been killed by weapons which exploded tunnels through their flesh. There might be other and more terrible devices . . .

The small army went on as quietly and as alertly as they could. They'd seen a light. It was now gone. They looked to their weapons, making sure the cold had not ruined their action by freezing some overlooked trace of lubricant. Only graphite could be used to lubricate metal at temperatures like this. The automatic weapons carried explosive bullets, with one bullet in four a tracer. But here were the firmest of possible orders that there was to be no firing at machinery. The whole purpose of this appallingly desperate raid was to capture—or at least for Hackett to see—one of the broadcast-power generators that supplied half the broadcast power which was three-quarters of all the power used on Earth.

It was the most hair-raising gamble ever made by human beings since history began. Its only justification was the stupidity of humans in allowing our power networks to become useless since the Greks arrival, and our steam generators to become unusable. Even the hydraulic generators were unused and their reservoirs half-emptied for irrigation. And men had seized so avidly upon power to be taken from the air that the loss of the broadcast supply would bring all human communications to a stop. Electrified railroads couldn't begin to move again before starvation swept the world. There were ships at sea which would become derelicts. Even ships which came to harbor and their docks could be unloaded only by hand, and the distribution of their cargoes would be so limping and so halting and inadequate that there was no city in which famine would not immediately appear.

But this had to be risked because if only the Greks could distribute power, the Greks had power of life and death over mankind. Which they would use. Which they had been invited and implored to return and use. Therefore men of former authority had very desperately and secretly set up this raid, because the great public believed in the Greks; because it could not be persuaded that their benevolence was a sham; because most men did not want to be independent of the Greks—they wanted to be their pensioners.

But there was that necessary few who gambled their lives and ours together with all the future of the race, because otherwise the gamble would be lost.

There came a time when, advancing with the greatest possible caution over snow between towering cliffs of stone, there were disturbances of the normal surface. The party of snowshoe-wearing men were groping as nearly as possible in the line along which the momentary light had been seen. A man at the end of the staggering advance felt firmness underfoot. The snow had been packed there, and he passed the word to the man next to him. A lieutenant of infantry made every man stop where he stood. With Hackett, who should have stayed behind until the others were successful or dead, he went ploughing across the snowfield to the spot.

There was semi-solidity under the snow. There were depressions where the snow had been packed. Something had pressed it down.

They fumbled about in the darkness. Only fifty yards away the sheer, overhanging mass of a pinnacled cliff blotted out half the sky. From somewhere near here a light had been visible an hour ago. Hackett and the lieutenant of infantry tramped back and forth. The packed snow was not all footprints. Here it had been compacted by a solid object of considerable size and weight.

Hackett began to feel cold chills running up and down his spine. His skin crawled at the back of his neck. This was almost certainly the landing place of the thing—whatever it was—that had come down from the moon and gone away again. If so, the power generator of the Greks was nearby. The aliens who intended the enslavement of Earth were close, with weapons that could only be guessed at, and who would certainly be as merciless to men as to their enslaved Aldarians.

The thing that made Hackett feel desperate was a feeling that the window from which the light had shone might open and pour pitiless light upon himself and his companions. The Greks would violently resent their presence. At any instant any conceivable weapon might open on them. They would be exterminated and the fact that humans were suspicious would be revealed, as well as the fact that they dared attack Greks . . .

There were lesser concretions under the snow. They were foot tracks. The snow was compacted as if the Greks and Aldarians had passed many times between the thing from the moon and—somewhere else.

The word passed in whispers. And then the very small army moved as skirmishers against the cliff base. They reached it without alarm. Hackett and the lieutenant fumbled for the end of that unseen packed trail.

Here was certainly a secret installation of the Greks—a matter of vast importance. They'd chosen a spot where very probably no human being had ever set foot. The secrecy of their construction of the installation was absolute. Their ability to hoodwink humanity had been demonstrated beyond any question, so they reacted exactly as men would have done under the same circumstances. All rational beings will act as fools when the circumstances favor that activity. The Greks, having reason for confidence, reacted with arrogance.

They left the installation to Aldarians to operate. Aldarians were there to turn off the power generator when or if the Greks wished it. And it did not occur to the Greks to set up intruder alarms in an unvisited wilderness which never had been and never ought to be approached by men.

Hackett found an opening in the rock. It was a door. Guns ready, he and the others entered it in single file. A very dimly lighted passage led upward. Presently there was a vast clear space, indifferently lighted, where the floor had been filled in with broken rock and the top roofed over. There would be snow upon that roof, now, and no examination from the air would show it. Besides, this was now the arctic night.

In the center of the artificial cavern there was a motionless, glittering, faintly droning complex of metal. It did not seem large enough to generate the power it did, and at that much of its apparent substance was jimcrackery. The Greks were habitual liars. They concealed the actual simplicity of their apparatus even when none but Greks and Aldarians should ever see it.

The rest of the cavern was bare rock. Here was nothing of civilization, of comfort, or of luxury men imagined as existing among the Greks. This was merely a rocky cave with a floor of packed stone. There were structures of metal pipe very much like bunk racks for use by people with little care for comfort. There was an undisturbed heap of parcels which looked like supplies. Except for the brazen mass of motionless machine in the center, the effect was much like that of a stable. Which it was—for those domestic animals, the Aldarians.

And there was one Aldarian in sight, seated on something indefinite, his furry head sunk into his hands in a position of absolute despair.

A foot scraped on a stone. He did not hear. Men filed into the cave. He did not notice. But then some motion somewhere in the tail of his eye roused him. He jerked his head about and saw them. Instantly he leaped up and as instantly Hackett knew he was terrified, with a terror past the fear of death. He did not flee. He snatched out a weapon from somewhere and leaped toward the machinery in the center of the cave.

Hackett did not fire. Instead, he flung the service automatic in his hand. The Aldarian was obviously under orders to destroy the machine rather than let men see it. He scrambled for it desperately. One of Hackett's followers snapped his rifle to his shoulder, but he did not pull the trigger. He did not need to.

The spinning automatic pistol hit the Aldarian with the impact of a pile driver. He was literally stopped in his tracks by the blow. And then there were men rushing to fling themselves upon him and make him fast.

Hackett snapped orders. Men spread out to hunt for other passages, other rooms, and other Aldarians. But most of them stayed to protect the mass of motionless machine until the entire installation was in their hands.

But there was no more. This one cavern was all there was. It was bare, it was chilly, it was comfortless. Half the broadcast power used on Earth depended on the machine it contained, but it had been made for Aldarians to occupy. Aldarians were slaves. Worse, they were domestic animals, and there was no thought of comfort for them.

But there was only one furry alien in the secret power-generating station.

That was one mystery, and there were others. But Hackett sent a man out to the dog teams and the Eskimos who had been ordered to stay out of the way if fighting started. There had been no fighting. The Eskimos were peacefully asleep and their dogs lay peacefully in the snow, some dozing but the more ambitious ones trying persistently to get rid of the muzzles which kept them from barking or fighting with their fellow dog team members.

That one messenger unlimbered the packed-away shortwave set. He made a call, waited for a reply and then gave a single code-word message. It meant incredible success. It was not wise, of course, to say anything informative in the clear. Too many humans were rejoicing because the Greks were on the way back to Earth.

But within minutes of the transmission of that one-word message, planes far away rumbled and took to the air, helicopters began to throb their way from the airstrip on Baffin Land, and very many others things began to happen. For one, planes began to carry equipment southward, past the equator and the torrid zone and to the remotest edges of the inhabited antarctic.

Hackett prowled around the huge masses of metal in the cavern. He scowled, examined, and drove his brains to superhuman effort. He wished that Lucy were present. For all of an hour he was subject to baffled bewilderment.

Then something fitted itself to something else, and that fitted . . .

The troopers who'd risked so much for so little excitement stared at him as he began to sputter furiously. He had solved the problem of the power generator. And it was infuriating—it was intolerable! It was enough to fill any man with rage to see how elementary, how utterly simple the whole thing was. He'd spent years with the possibility right under his nose, so to speak, and hadn't realized it.

It was power unlimited under absolute control. It was energy inexhaustible without harmful radiation or even high temperatures to get out of hand. The Greks had found it. They'd made use of it. They'd built a civilization upon it. But that civilizaton was in their own image, and the Greks were not nice people.

There was a curious parallel, in the discovery of one principle that would shape a culture, to the human discovery of the principle of the dynamo. When Faraday discovered that a current-carrying wire in a magnetic field moved sideways, he began the sequence of events which determined human technology. Monstrous atomic-powered generators—no more were built after the coming of the Greks—to microvolto-meters and incandescent lights, the things of which mankind made most use were invariably dependent upon that principle for their use, or in their manufacture, or in their distribution. The one observation was responsible for human technology as far as it had gone. The Grek discovery was different, that was all. It was different, and therefore the technology and the civilization growing from it were different from that of Earth.

But of course the Greks were different, too.

Presently there were planes circling over a place on previously unknown Morrow Island, parachutes blossomed in the night, and flares destroyed the darkness at the earth's surface. Presently Hackett was again explaining disgustedly to newly-arrived eminent scientists what was so plainly to be seen, and they doubted and objected and grew indignant—and then suddenly understood and were stunned by what they realized.

Lucy arrived. She was prim, but her eyes shone. She explained that she'd been working with the Aldarian nerve current device and had found a way to project it in a beam. She was sure that if a really powerful nerve stimulus field could be beamed at Aldarians, that *if* the sounds produced in their severed hearing nerves could be made intelligible . . .

There were high level scientists feverishly anxious to get back to their laboratories to get to work. There were others arriving to have their skepticism satisfied. There were men demanding facts of Hackett so they could begin to make this and that . . .

And back home somebody had blown up half a ploughed field with an Aldarian device modified to do something unknown. It turned out be the violent breakdown of all endothermal compounds. Somebody near Denver had stumbled on a particular shaping of the pointed end of the fishlike Grek device part, and it pushed down walls with no reverse thrust on the device. It was a so-far-primitive space drive, which only needed to be worked out in detail to make rockets mere souvenirs of a quaint, old-fashioned period.

But there was one man who'd worked zestfully in his own field, quite alone and with no help from anything Hackett or anybody else had accomplished. He'd studied the gesture code of the Greks and Aldarians, in motion pictures taken when they were away from the ship. He'd studied pictures showing gesture conversations taking place before an Aldarian writing down something for humans to read. This signal language student had the text of the writings and had learned to talk in gesture code, though with an extremely limited vocabulary. There was some similarity to the sign language of American Indians, who might not know a word of each others' spoken language, but could discuss all sorts of subjects in detail by signs.

Hackett assigned him to establish communication with the solitary Aldarian captured in the Morrow Island cavern. He and Lucy went back together to arrange the next two stages in a sequence which would be more hair-raising in each incident.

He held conferences. Most of the world celebrated or gloated that the Greks were coming back. They'd said so. But Hackett and a certain number of close-mouthed individuals made plans and preparations that would have gotten them lynched anywhere on the globe.

There was a garage mechanic who'd repaired a sinter-field generator much too well, so that even metals crumbled to powder when it was turned on them. In on this discussion was a general of ordnance, an electrical engineer with some reputation for designing gigantic dynamo-electric machinery, and the head of an electrical workers' union.

There was discussion with linguists and semanticists and communications experts. Their subject matter had to be referred to Lucy with an ultimate referral to the man who'd studied Grek-Aldarian gesture-codes. He and the captured Aldarian were flown back to where communication as achieved could be put on tape, and the tape applied to control an Aldarian hearing aid magnified and made able to transmit its field directionally.

There was a conference. They were innumerable, but Hackett did happen to be the man who as of now thought more lucidly about Grek-style devices and principles than anybody else. He assumed the authority to insist that he was going with the expedition to the antarctic. That expedition had the tightest of possible schedules. It would have to shave minutes to reach Antarctica, do what it must do there and get back to the landing cradle in Ohio before the Grek ship came to ground a second time.

In this seething activity, some curious sidelights turned up. The delegation which had implored the return of the Greks somehow gathered bunting and flags and motortrucks and fuel—the fuel was an achievement—and headed for the landing cradle to prepare a welcoming ceremony for those philanthropists of space, the Greks. The Aldarians instructing male and female students in the sciences of the Greks were unaware of any change in the prospective sequence of events. One Aldarian at the dummy power-station Hackett had entered bitterly gave up hope that human beings might turn out to be wiser or stronger than the Greks, so he and his people might some day hope to be more than slaves. And some thousands of tons of gold bullion accumulated at the Mediterranean station where sea water was de-salted to be pumped into the Sahara basin. There was much pilfering of that gold by workmen at the plant, but nobody else, anywhere, wanted it.

Then, when Hackett found that he had to abandon further efforts of any sort in order to head for the airport for the journey south, a large man with a patient expression came into the office he'd preempted.

"Well?" said Hackett. "I don't mean to be impolite, but I have to get going—"

The large man said mildly, "I came to wish you good luck. I think it's important that you have it."

"Thanks and all that, but—"

"We've a mutual acquaintance," said the large man. "A Miss Constance Thale, who went to school with me. She wrote me a very pleasant note the other day. I understand that you and Doctor Thale are to be married. She thought I might be interested. I telephoned her once about you."

Hackett blinked. Then he said hastily, "I suppose I should apologize for giving orders and such things without authority, but they more or less—"

"You've no idea," said the large man mildly, "how pleased I am when people don't insist that I pass on everything they want to do, when what they're doing is sensible, that is." Then he said; "I'm really hopeful now. The credit will have to be distributed rather widely if things go as we want them to, but—You're ready to go? I'll drive you to the airport."

Hackett and Lucy, waiting below, were driven to the airport in a White House limousine, which would be beautifully calculated to give pleasure to Lucy's Cousin Constance when she was free to talk about it. And they took off for Antarctica.

The look of things at their landing place was singularly unlike the darkness and gloom of Baffin Land and Morrow Island. There was sunlight. Ice was blindingly white. Open water was incredibly blue. An atomic submarine waited with atomic-headed rockets ready to take over the enterprise if unhappily the expeditionary force should fail.

From the moment of their landing to the climax of their journey, this was altogether different from the Morrow Island effort. For one thing, exploration of Antarctica was a continuing process. There were still hundreds of thousands of square miles no human eye had ever seen, but the continent had a relatively permanent population of as much as two hundred persons. They moved on fixed routes as a rule, but they did move about. Snow tractors were routine in some areas, and there were caches of fuel along lines sometimes hundreds of miles in length, though they might run alongside the bases of mountains whose other sides were totally unknown. Planes were not unprecedented here. So if there were a Grek power-generating station on Antarctica it would undoubtedly be more carefully hidden than at the other end of the world, but aliens in it would be less likely to imagine every visible movement directed against them.

Snow tractors carried the expedition inland. In the tractor carrying the nerve-stimulus beam projector, Lucy gave Hackett a rundown of progress in race-to-race communication.

"That poor Aldarian you captured," she observed, "was absolutely pitiable, Jim. Do you know why he was alone?"

Hackett shook his head.

"You hurried back," she said. "But after you left they found there'd been some others. They'd been killed and dumped in snowdrifts. Something had come down from the moon. Greks. Just before their ship took off from Earth they made a discovery they didn't like. So while humans got to miss them, they made a surprise inspection on the Morrow Island station. They found an Aldarian hearing aid. So they killed four of the five Aldarians who'd been there, and promised the last that half of those on the ship who were hostages for him would be killed. Half. You see? He was punished by the killing of some hostages. But he couldn't think of revenge because there were more. They could kill the rest."

"I see," said Hackett. His tone was detached. "I don't like the Greks. I hope things go our way when they land again."

Lucy shivered a little. "He was so completely desperate that I think he'd have killed himself when he got the chance. You see, in being captured or even killed he'd have committed a crime in the eyes of the Greks!"

"Nice people, the Greks," said Hackett ironically. "Nice!"

"So by the time the sign language man came to try to talk to him, he was already due for absolutely every punishment the Greks could inflict. So he talked. He was brought down and showed the things that are being got ready. Did anybody tell you how a stepped-up sinter beam makes metal fall to powder?"

"Yes," said Hackett. "I know about it."

"He began to hope we might kill some Greks, so he told us everything he could. We fixed up a hearing aid so he could hear his own voice and he made a recording. The transmitter in the back can send it so that Aldarians with cut hearing nerves will hear the language they used when they could talk like anybody else."

"You'll broadcast it, and it'll urge the Aldarians to turn against the Greks?"

"Not—not too soon," said Lucy unhappily. "The Aldarian you captured said if we used it too soon some of them would think it was a Grek trick and not dare believe it. And they'd tell the Greks for safety's sake."

"I repeat," said Hackett evenly, "that I don't like the Greks."

She was silent for a little while. The tractor groaned and rumbled upon and through the snow. Then she said, "He said that from now on the Greks won't wait to make Aldarians deaf. They'll cut their hearing nerves while they're babies, so they'll never have any idea of sound or spoken words."

The tractor went on and on. There were many others before it and others behind. The art of traveling over a continent of snow and ice was well developed. The sun moved around the horizon, never dipping below it. There came a time when rest was necessary. They halted. They slept. With insufficient sleep they went on again.

Back in the United States there was a further communication from the Greks to the volunteer Aldarians patiently teaching nonsense to aspiring students.

It announced that the Grek ship would descend at the same earth cradle that had been prepared for their ship before. They'd known of the atomic bombs planted there before their first landing. It was a form of arrogance to use it again, ignoring the possibility that humans could devise any weapon they could not counter.

"They're plenty confident," said Hackett when he heard of it. "If they should be right, by the time they administer punishment to those of us who've been working to defy them—"

"We'll be dead," said Lucy firmly. "We'll make sure of it."

"If they have the least suspicion," said Hackett grimly, "we'll be wiped out tomorrow. You, by the way, will stay at least three miles back from where any fighting happens."

Lucy did not answer.

The day's journey continued. The sun did not ever set, but its rays were low and slanting. During this day, a plane flew low overhead and dropped an object by parachute. It was a packet of high altitude photographs of the terrain all around the place to which the thing from the moon had descended and from which it had risen again. The pictures were incredibly detailed. From thirty-five thousand feet they showed square miles of cracked and fissured surface, and a range of mountains with every valley revealed to the last jagged boulder which penetrated the snow. There was a mark calling attention to one place on one enlarged photographic print.

It was a depression in the snow, where something heavy had packed the soft stuff down. The low-slanting sunshine cast shadows in the depressed space.

There was discussion. Painstaking examination told more. There was a hundred-foot line of trampled snow from the single large depression. As on Morrow Island, the thing from the moon had landed here, as near as possible to this hidden power-generating station. It had only been necessary to walk thirty yards through the snow. The Greks, evidently, did not imagine a

race of such variegated talents that it could find footprints in snow, hundreds of miles from any human
settlement, made by aliens marching to and from an
object that humans should be unable to detect.

The expedition sent a tight microwave beam skyward to where the plane that had dropped the pictures now circled out of sight. The plane went away.
The expedition went on. There was a schedule to be
kept to. It was necessary if efforts now preparing
elsewhere were to take effect on the exact instant for
the exact effect for the tractors to take advantage of.

The ground party went on in its unending, jolting,
crawling progress. At nine hundred hours it moved
toward a mountain range from whose farther side it
could not be seen. At nine hundred forty hours planes
came flying low above the snow surface. They were
medium bomber jets, capable of a speed of mach two
at sea level, and carrying bombs of very respectable
size. They had come down from the United States,
refueled and now they plunged over the tractor expedition too fast for the eye to follow. They were a
muttering to the rear. They were a bellowing overhead. Then they were a diminishing uproar ahead.
The sound of their going trailed them by miles.

They lifted sharply to clear mountain bridges and
dipped down; there were ripping, bursting bombs,
and a cloud of white phosphorus smoke began to form
to windward of the mountains' farther slopes. There
was another tumult overhead. Hackett was almost
deafened by this, because he'd plunged out of the
tractor carrying Lucy and was insisting upon climb-
ing into another.

A second squadron of bombers went racing across
the snow sheet and steeply upward. More bombs
thudded as they landed. The mountains echoed to
sounds they had never heard before in all their millions of years.

And the snow tractors, abruptly dumping all excess
loads, flung into the highest speed of which they were
capable and raced toward a spot where some unknown
object had marked the snow exactly as the snow had

been marked on Morrow Island half a world away.

It was not spectacular. From a distance it seemed only that there were small white-painted dots moving over snowfields and the lower slopes of mountains. They left tracks in the snow behind them. Now some of them plunged into dense clouds of white vapor moving slowly toward them from where five-hundred-pound and larger smoke bombs had landed. More of them dived into the white-out the smoke bombs made. Presently there was only one such dot remaining away from the blank whiteness from which detonations and the rasping of automatic weapons came.

The moment arrived when the tractor in which Hackett rode could go no farther. With others, he plunged out and made his way ahead. There were other vehicles still moving. There was dense fog. There were explosions . . .

Shrilling whistles and shouts called to all men. Hackett, panting, ran for the source of the outcry. There was a blown-away door and a cavern from which warm air floated out. Hackett dived into it, with many others. They swarmed down passages. This was no such stable-like cave as the arctic one had been. He saw an Aldarian. The Aldarian had his back against a stony wall and his arms spread wide. This was what the broadcast by Lucy's tractor—inaudible to Greks and men alike—had warned was to be a signal by Aldarians that they wanted to strike a blow at the Greks. This furry man held the pose, but he jerked his head fiercely, mouthing unintelligible sounds, urging the humans into a certain passage on beyond.

Hackett tore into it. There was an Aldarian who fought desperately against the invading humans. He had to be killed. There were others who hesitated. Hackett saw one weeping as he tried to decide instantly between terror for those who were hostages for him, and the ravening, raging, horrible longing to strike at the race of Greks.

There was a flash of flame past Hackett's face. It splashed against stone and glowing powder and pebbles dropped down. Hackett fired. There were other men with him. They were in a room of such spaciousness and lavish luxury as no human despot ever had made for himself. And there was a bulky, gray-skinned Grek moving swiftly toward apparatus at its end. He fired once more and the flash of his hand weapon was like lightning. He had almost reached the device which was plainly a communicator of some sort—

Hackett killed him, from ten yards, with a .45 caliber, primitive, automatic smokeless-powder pistol.

And again, later, there were planes flying overhead and parachutes blooming in the sky. But it was day, here. It would be day for a long while yet. The sun wouldn't set for some six weeks to come, and then it would set only briefly.

This was forty-eight hours before the Grek ship returned to Earth. When it did turn up, it didn't appear as a silver speck beyond the nearer planets, increasing slowly in size as it came nearer. That might have been tactful, but the Greks did not think of it.

The Grek ship came casually out from behind the edge of the moon. It came deliberatly toward Earth. It was huge. It was monstrous. It is probable that the Greks sent calls to their two main installations on Earth. If so, there was no answer. But the enslaved Aldarians in the dummy broadcast transmitters replied promptly, and the Aldarians assigned to teach Grek science to human students were prompt to respond. That was enough. The Grek ship came on. It seems certain that there were no misgivings on board. The Greks knew the state of human civilization. The race of men was primitive in its development. Its technology was absurd. No human being was able to understand how any Grek machine worked. Compared to the Greks, men were savages! At least they had been less than two months before, and it would take millenia for them to overtake the Greks if they were allowed to try. But they wouldn't be.

Moreover, the human race had sent message after message, imploring the Greks to come back and direct them, guide them,—in effect, rule them. They would be docile, and if they ever developed ideas unlike their present tearful gratitude to and for all things Grek—

So the Grek ship came down. Where the enormous viewing-stands had been built for the ceremony of its departure, there were ragged flags and not much bunting and very few humans. But men knew well enough that they were unable to live without the Greks once they'd encountered them. Presently they would discover how promptly they'd die if they displeased them.

But just now there was the matter of landing.

The ship came down and down and down, and it was a monstrous, ungainly object. But it was beautifully controlled. It swung slightly to align itself perfectly with the scooped-out earthen cradle men had prepared for it eight months before. It was the length of five large city blocks, and its thickness was that of the height of a sixty-story building. It was more gigantic than any structure the human race had ever built on solid ground—and it roamed among the stars!

The delegation for welcoming the Greks back to Earth set up a shout of greeting. It was, as it happened, a very small sound in the vastness of the empty stands. But some of the delegates were weeping with joy that now everything would turn out all right with the wise, kind Greks to decide everything for them, and everybody would be rich and nobody would have to do anything in particular . . .

The Grek ship settled neatly and tidily and perfectly in the berth designed for it. Hackett and Lucy watched, Hackett with a surpassing grimness. A door began to open for someone to come out and be greeted by men who essayed to give the Earth and all its people into the benevolent and munificent hands of the Greks.

Then several things happened. They did not seem related, somehow, but they all happened at the same time and place. There were a dozen or so modified sinter-field generators under the grandstand. They

had been built after consultation with a garage mechanic who'd tried to mend such a generator of small
size when it was smashed in a truck-car collision.
These dozen sinter-field generators were changed from
the original model. They projected a beam instead of
a field, and in this stepped-up beam metal crumbled
to powder.

There were some super-laser-beam projectors, of
which the idea had come from a burned-out high
school science classroom. They would burn a hole
through half a mountainside if desired, and repeat the
blast with every alternation of the current supplied
them.

There were guided missiles carrying relatively miniature artillery shell atomic bombs. They developed
the destructive power of no more than five hundred
tons of chemical high explosive. And they could not
be inactivated. A small device like an Aldarian hearing aid made sure of the fact.

And there was a high power beam of the nerve
stimulus field, which could tell every Aldarian in the
ship, as if his hearing had been restored, that now
was the time to revolt.

It was quite odd that all these things went into
operation at once. All of them were strictly focused
upon one particular part of the Grek ship. Oddly
enough that was the part of the ship reserved for
Greks, so certain captured Aldarians affirmed. There
was a great space between that infinitely luxurious
living space and the stable-like quarters reserved for
Aldarians—they being domestic animals only.

They all went into action at once, with no particularly dramatic preface. But the first three hundred
feet of the ship shivered and billowed downward and
out. It had suddenly become metallic powder, nothing
more. As it fell, from the height of a fifty-story human
building, intolerably brilliant laser-beams flashed into
it like so many lightning bolts, at sixty bolts to the
second and with a dozen projectors flinging them.

There was only one guided missile used. It went
off, of course. It scattered metal dust far and wide,

and proved conclusively that there were no more
Greks left alive in the ship. Further bombardment
would have been undesirable. Technical reasons aside,
there were very nearly two thousand Aldarian slaves
in the ship. They were the technicians and the scientists responsible for the ship and all its capabilities.
The Greks specialized in ruling, in slave-owning. It
turned out to be a weakness. The Aldarians, when
they found they were free, only regretted very, very
bitterly that no Greks had been left alive so they could
kill them.

But even they found some small satisfaction in the
fact that the instruments used to destroy the Grek
ship had been, in the last analysis, only variations on
the devices the Greks had brought to Earth as gifts.

Everybody knows, of course, what happened after
that. The destruction of the Grek ship ended immediately all fond notions of pie in the sky and working
one day a week and all the rest. But, rather strangely,
we seemed to feel that something else was more important after we'd learned and digested the lessons
to be drawn from the things the Aldarians told us.
We went back to work. Resolutely. We who went
through the coming of the Greks were like the humans
of today. We could be fools, but also we could be
something more.

When we heard the story of the Aldarians, we were
enraged. We liked the Aldarians. A fine high sense
of mission came to us. We immediately resolved that
Earth must be protected against the chance of another Grek ship coming to Earth with plans about
our liberty and the futures of our children. We began
grimly to build ships of space to protect them. The
Aldarians helped with strictly practical information
and aid, besides. We acquired a space fleet.

And we continued to learn from the Aldarians. The
Greks were liars. There were no thousands of civilized planets in the Nurmi cluster. In fact, the Greks
didn't come from there. There was no organized interstellar commerce, with gigantic ships plying from

world to world upon their lawful occasions. There were civilized planets, yes. But there were Greks. And the Greks were not a civilization. Centuries or millenia gone by, they'd made some discoveries. They built space ships. They searched for colonizable planets. They found partly civilized ones instead. So they changed their plans. They conquered them and ruled them.

When on a given world there ceased to be slaves by thousands or tens of thousands for each individual Grek, they had their slaves build them a ship and some of them searched for another habitable, partly civilized world to be conquered and ruled. The Aldarians had been victims. There'd been others. Earth, by all the rules of reason, should have been a victim, too. But the Greks would be our deadly enemies if they ever learned we'd destroyed a Grek ship. If Earth could defend itself, it was dangerous!

So, we did what we saw was necessary. We sent a ship to the home planet of the Aldarians. Some of the Aldarians we'd freed were on board. There were Greks ruling that world. We took the necessary action. Then there were no more Greks there—and Earth had an ally and men had staunch and grateful friends.

Then that first ship went exploring. It found a habitable planet not occupied by any but lower animals. We decided to colonize it. But it had to be protected against Greks! So we began to hunt for them. We found worlds with Grek masters ruling millions of slaves. We took action. We found more desirable, colonizable worlds . . .

All of this is tediously well-known. The Earth space fleet is large and competent, and our spacemen are welcome visitors on all the worlds which are now our allies. Interstellar trade has been developing admirably, and as long as our fleet can be said to rule the ether waves, we can look forward to an indefinitely long period of peace and prosperity for ourselves and the other races we have rescued or protect.

But we who remember the coming of the Greks to Earth are sometimes scoffed at by later generations.

We find it hard to explain to them how terrifying the coming of the ship was, and why we behaved as we did. We *did* act like idiots! But all men can, given the opportunity.

What we sometimes suspect is that maybe, some day, our descendants will be fools, too, only in a different way. Suppose, for instance, that a man-manned ship finds a desirable new planet, far out of the normal range of our ships. And suppose there's a semicivilized race on it. Suppose this human ship comes casually out from behind that planet's moon, and waits to see what the planet's inhabitants will do. And suppose that presently it pieces together a vocabulary of those barbarian's words, and says that it will be very happy to pass on such technical information as the aborigines can make use of, and therefore it asks permission to land . . .

Heaven help us, it could happen! So we who remember the coming of the Greks hammer at later generations, trying to make them see that they mustn't be the same kind of fools we were. Or the Greks were. Or the Aldarians. Or the—

It seems to be true that all the intelligent races of our galaxy are capable of acting like fools if the conditions are right. That is, we can all be idiots under proper encouragement. So—

Don't do it! Don't do it! Don't!

(For the record, it should be mentioned that James Hackett, Ph.D., and Lucy Thale, M.D., were married within a month after the destruction of the Grek ship. The bride was given away by the President of the United States and the maid of honor was Miss Constance Thale. The most authoritative information is to the effect that they are engaged in living happily ever after.)

TOP SCIENCE FICTION
FROM MACFADDEN-BARTELL